PROBLEM SOLVING: GRADES 3-4
TABLE OF CONTENTS

INTRODUCTION

The National Council of Teachers of Mathematics (NCTM) has set specific standards to help students become confident of their mathematical abilities. Communicating mathematically and problem solving are the keys to helping students develop skills to apply in their daily lives and in later careers.

Based on the belief that students learn to reason mathematically in order to become problem solvers, the strategies in this book show students more than one way to solve problems. These strategies are not absolute techniques, however. Learning a multitude of ways to approach a problem is part of the philosophy in developing sets of problem-solving strategies.

ORGANIZATION

The first chapter, Working with Numbers, is a review for students at this level who may need additional practice. The other nine chapters offer several strategies to solve a given type of problem: Addition, Subtraction, Multiplication, Division, Mixed Operations, Fractions, Decimals and Money, Measurement, and Logic. Each lesson begins with an introductory problem which is solved using a series of clearly defined steps. The practice problems are based on real-life situations and demonstrate use of this set of steps to reach a solution.

SPECIAL FEATURE

Each chapter concludes with a "Math Madness" activity page that presents an opportunity for students to choose their own strategy to solve problems. The character Harriet the Handy Woman is featured on each of these pages. Harriet provides the students with a unique way to approach the challenges. Divergent thinking is promoted in these lessons.

The following problem-solving strategies are demonstrated:

CHOOSE AN OPERATION Students determine which operation (addition, subtraction, multiplication, or division) to use based on the information presented.

ESTIMATION Students learn both when and how to estimate answers, based on rounding numbers and performing the appropriate operation. Estimation is encouraged as a strategy in all problem solving to verify reasonableness of answers.

FIND A PATTERN This strategy emphasizes pattern recognition of given sequences of numbers, geometric shapes, pictorial information, and other data for problem solving.

GUESS AND CHECK Students learn a variety of methods to reduce the number of trial and error efforts needed to reach accuracy in answers.

IDENTIFY EXTRA OR MISSING INFORMATION By identifying pertinent information, students learn to recognize information which is extra or missing.

MAKE A DRAWING Creating visual images of information makes analysis of the facts easier.

MAKE A LIST Students learn to organize information into meaningful lists for later matching or computation.

MAKE A TABLE Pattern recognition, identification of extra or missing information, and arrangement of data into a visual form demonstrate the effectiveness of making a table.

USE A GRAPH Graphing organizes information so that comparisons can be made visually.

MULTI-STEP PROBLEMS Some complex problems require the completion of more than one step to calculate the solution. This strategy emphasizes the importance of identifying both the given information and the order of operations to reach the solution.

USE LOGIC As it implies, using logic is similar to

using common sense. In this strategy students learn to recognize relationships and to answer the question, "Does it make sense?" Strategies include a process of elimination of answers and visual representation of information to organize the elements of a problem.

WORK BACKWARDS This section introduces a strategy for solving complex problems in which the end result is given. By recognizing clue words and using them to solve the problem, students can work backwards from an answer. This skill develops background for later success in algebra.

WRITE A NUMBER SENTENCE Converting written statements into numerical sentences to solve for an unknown is the basis of an algebraic approach. This strategy demonstrates identification of known and unknown information to develop sentences for solutions.

USE

This book is designed for independent use by students who have had instruction in the specific skills covered in these lessons. Copies of the activities can be given to individuals, pairs of students, or small groups for completion. They can also be used as a center activity. If students are familiar with the content, the worksheets can be homework for reviewing and reinforcing problem-solving concepts.

To begin, determine the implementation that fits your students' needs and your classroom structure. The following plan suggests a format for this implementation:

1. Explain the purpose of the worksheets to your class.
2. Review the mechanics of how you want students to work with the exercises.
3. Review the specific skill for the students who may not remember the process for successful completion of the computation.
4. Introduce students to the process and to the

purpose of the activities. Distribute the Letter to Students.
5. Do a practice activity together.
6. Allow students to experiment, discover, and explore a variety of ways to solve a given problem.

Additional Notes

1. Parent Communication. Send the Letter to Parents home with students, and encourage students to share the Letter to Students with their parents.
2. Bulletin Board. Display completed worksheets to show student progress.
3. Center Activities. Use the worksheets as center activities to give students the opportunity to work cooperatively.
4. Class Record. Duplicate the grid sheets found on pages 7–9. Record student names in the left column. Note date of completion of each lesson for each student.
5. Have fun. Working with these activities can be fun as well as meaningful for you and your students.

Dear Parent,

During this school year, our class will be working with mathematical problem solving strategies. To increase your child's problem solving skills, we will be completing activity sheets that provide practice to ensure mastery of these important skills.

From time to time, I may send home activity sheets. To best help your child, please consider the following suggestions:

- Provide a quiet place to work.
- Go over the directions and the sample exercises together.
- Encourage your child to do his or her best.
- Check the lesson when it is complete.
- Go over your child's work, and note improvements as well as concerns.

Help your child maintain a positive attitude about problem solving activities. Let your child know that each lesson provides an opportunity to have fun and to learn. If your child expresses anxiety about these strategies, help him or her understand what causes the stress. Then talk about ways to eliminate math anxiety.

Above all, enjoy this time you spend with your child. He or she will feel your support, and skills will improve with each activity completed.

Thank you for your help!

Cordially,

Name _____ Date _____

Dear Student:

    This year you will be working with problem solving strategies in mathematics. You're wondering how well you'll do. Math problem solving is an important skill, and sometimes people feel anxious if they don't understand right away. The activities will help you practice so you can feel more confident about working math problems. You will be reviewing many strategies with sample problems and working some word problems on your own. These activities will show you a fun way to learn problem solving.

As you complete the worksheets, remember the following:
- Read the directions carefully.
- Study the sample problems, and follow the steps for each strategy.
- Read each question carefully.
- Check your answers after you complete a problem.

    You will learn many ways to solve math problems. Have fun as you develop these skills!

STUDENT NAME	CHAPTER 1								CHAPTER 2								CHAPTER 3								CHAPTER 4							
	1	2	3	4	5	6	7	8	1	2	3	4	5	6	7	8	1	2	3	4	5	6	7	8	1	2	3	4	5	6	7	8

Problem Solving 3-4, SV 6759-X

STUDENT NAME	CHAPTER 5								CHAPTER 6								CHAPTER 7								CHAPTER 8							
	1	2	3	4	5	6	7	8	1	2	3	4	5	6	7	8	1	2	3	4	5	6	7	8	1	2	3	4	5	6	7	8

Problem Solving 3-4, SV 6759-X

STUDENT NAME	CHAPTER 9								CHAPTER 10								COMMENTS
	1	2	3	4	5	6	7	8	1	2	3	4	5	6	7	8	

Correlation to the NCTM Standards for grades K - 4

These charts indicate the specific mathematics skills incorporated in the activities in this guide correlated to the National Council for Teachers of Mathematics (NCTM) Standards for grades K - 4.

	Unit 1	Unit 2	Unit 3	Unit 4	Unit 5	Unit 6	Unit 7	Unit 8	Unit 9	Unit 10
MATHEMATICS AS PROBLEM SOLVING										
Use problem-solving approach . . .	X	X	X	X	X	X	X	X	X	X
Formulate problems . . .		X	X	X	X	X	X	X	X	X
Develop and apply strategies . . .	X	X	X	X	X	X	X	X	X	X
Verify and interpret results . . .		X	X	X	X	X	X	X	X	X
Acquire confidence . . .		X	X	X	X	X	X	X	X	X
MATHEMATICS AS COMMUNICATION										
Relate physical materials, pictures . . .	X	X	X	X	X	X	X	X	X	
Reflect on and clarify their own thinking . . .		X	X	X	X	X				
Relate their everyday language . . .	X	X	X	X				X	X	X
Realize that representing, discussing . . .		X	X		X	X	X	X	X	
MATHEMATICS AS REASONING										
Draw logical conclusions . . .		X	X	X		X			X	X
Use models, known facts . . .		X	X	X	X	X	X	X		X
Justify their answers . . .				X		X			X	X
Use patterns and relationships . . .	X	X	X	X	X	X			X	
Believe that mathematics makes sense . . .				X		X		X	X	
MATHEMATICAL CONNECTIONS										
Link conceptual and procedural . . .		X	X		X		X	X	X	
Relate various representations of concepts . . .					X		X		X	X
Recognize relationships among different topics . . .					X					X
Use mathematics in other curriculum . . .									X	
Use mathematics in their daily lives . . .	X	X	X	X	X	X	X	X	X	X
ESTIMATION										
Explore estimation strategies . . .		X	X	X	X	X		X	X	
Recognize when an estimate . . .				X		X		X		
Determine the reasonableness . . .				X		X		X	X	
Apply estimation . . .		X	X	X	X	X		X		
NUMBER SENSE & NUMERATION										
Construct number meanings through real-world experiences . . .	X			X		X		X	X	X
Understand our numeration system . . .	X			X		X				
Develop number sense . . .	X		X	X	X	X				
Interpret the multiple uses . . .				X		X				
CONCEPTS OF WHOLE NUMBER OPERATIONS										
Develop meaning for the operations . . .	X	X	X	X	X	X		X	X	
Relate the mathematical language . . .		X	X	X	X	X		X	X	
Recognize that a wide variety of problem . . .				X	X	X		X	X	
Develop operation sense . . .	X	X	X	X	X	X		X	X	

STANDARD 1 — MATHEMATICS AS PROBLEM SOLVING
STANDARD 2 — MATHEMATICS AS COMMUNICATION
STANDARD 3 — MATHEMATICS AS REASONING
STANDARD 4 — MATHEMATICAL CONNECTIONS
STANDARD 5 — ESTIMATION
STANDARD 6 — NUMBER SENSE & NUMERATION
STANDARD 7 — CONCEPTS OF WHOLE NUMBER OPERATIONS

ASSESSMENT, page 2

For questions 5-6, find and draw a line through the extra information in the problem. Then solve the problem.

5. Joy plays basketball for the Panthers. On Monday Joy scored 27 points. On Friday she scored 15 points. Joy's best friend scored 13 points on Friday. How many total points did Joy score in the two days?

_____

6. The pet store has 8 puppies and 7 kittens. It also has 9 sizes of dog and cat collars. How many puppies and kittens are at the store?

_____

For questions 7-8, round to the nearest hundred, then estimate to solve the problem.

7. There were 2,349 people watching the parade. Then it started to rain, so 542 people went home. About how many people stayed to watch the parade?

_____

8. There are 1,115 students at Lincoln School. Lee School has 984 students. About how many more students attend Lincoln than Lee?

_____

For questions 9-10, work backwards to solve each problem.

9. The pet shop sold 70 guppies last weekend. There were 532 guppies left. How many guppies did the pet shop have before the weekend?

_____

10. On Wednesday Aiko counted 132 goldfish in her tank. Tuesday she had added 47 fish to the tank. How many fish did she have before Tuesday?

_____

ASSESSMENT, page 3

For questions 11-12, choose an operation. Circle the correct operation, then solve the problem.

11. Many softball games were played at the picnic. There were 72 players. If each team has 9 members, how many teams were at the picnic?

$$\begin{array}{r} 7\,2 \\ \times\ \ 9 \\ \hline ?\,? \end{array}$$ $72 \div 9 = ?$

_____

12. There are 16 picnic tables at the park. Each table seats 8 people. How many people can sit at picnic tables?

$$\begin{array}{r} 1\,6 \\ \times\ \ 8 \\ \hline ?\,? \end{array}$$ $16 \div 8 = ?$

_____

For questions 13-14, use guess and check to solve each problem.

13. Toby's bag of apples weighs 8 pounds more than his bag of oranges. The two bags weigh 24 pounds total. How much does the bag of apples weigh?

_____

14. Toby and Travis are brothers. Toby is 3 years older than Travis. The sum of their ages is 37. How old is Toby?

_____

ASSESSMENT, page 3

For questions 15-16, use more than one step to solve each problem.

15. At the Party Shop, Liz bought 7 balloons at 28 cents each and 4 whistles at 33 cents each. She gave the clerk a $5.00 bill. How much change did she get?

_____

16. Jack bought 2 piñatas for a party. He gave the sales clerk $35.00 and received $3.80 change. How much did each piñata cost?

_____

For questions 17-18, write two <u>units</u> of measurement for each item.

17. A flagpole:

weight:_____   height:_____

18. A swimming pool:

length:_____   volume:_____

For questions 19-20, use logic to solve each problem.

19. Warren, Ilda, and John each ate a piece of pizza. One pizza is sausage, one is cheese, and one is mushroom. Warren had meat on his pizza. John is allergic to mushrooms. Who will eat the mushroom pizza?

_____

20. Blake, Alex, and Logan each hold a different color card in a card game. One card is blue, one is green, and one is red. Blake does not have a red card. Logan has the green card. Who has the red card?

_____

PUTTING THINGS IN THEIR PLACES

Every 2-digit number has a tens place and a ones place.

Count the groups of tens and ones.

tens	ones	
4	7	= 47

Every 3-digit number has a hundreds place, a tens place, and a ones place.

Count the groups of hundreds, tens, and ones.

hundreds	tens	ones	
1	6	3	= 163

Every 4-digit number has a thousands place, a hundreds place, a tens place, and a ones place.

Count the groups of thousands, hundreds, tens, and ones.

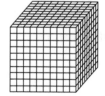

th	h	t	o	
1	3	4	2	= 1,342

GO ON TO NEXT PAGE

Name _____ Date _____

EVERYTHING IN ITS PLACE

Count the groups of tens and ones.
Then write the numerals.

tens	ones
4	8

= 48

1.

tens	ones

= _____

Count the groups of hundreds, tens, and ones.
Then write the numerals.

hundreds	tens	ones
1	2	7

= 127

2.

hundreds	tens	ones

= _____

Count the groups of thousands, hundreds, tens, and ones.
Then write the numerals.

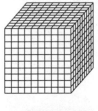

th	h	t	o
1	3	4	2

= 1,342

3.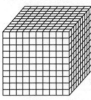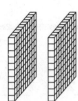

th	h	t	o

= _____

LINING THINGS UP

When adding numbers, start with the digits in the ones place. It helps to make a table.

Find 214 + 465

add the ones				add the tens				add the hundreds		
h	t	o		h	t	o		h	t	o
2	1	4		2	1	4		2	1	4
+ 4	6	5		+ 4	6	5		+ 4	6	5
		9			7	9		6	7	9

Now it's your turn! Make a table. Line up the numbers, then add.

1.

t	o		t	o
2	5		4	6
+	4		+	3
2	9			

```
  5 3        3 4        1 7        5 1 7
+ 4 2      + 5 5      + 5 4 2    + 1 6 2
```

Sometimes you have to regroup. Start with the digits in the ones place and regroup as needed.

Find 974 + 346

add the ones regroup				add the tens regroup				add the hundreds regroup			
h	t	o		h	t	o		th	h	t	o
		1			1	1		1	1	1	
9	7	4		9	7	4			9	7	4
+ 3	4	6		+ 3	4	6		+	3	4	6
		0			2	0		1	3	2	0

Make a table. Line up the numbers, then add. Regroup as needed.

2.

t	o		t	o
3	6		2	9
+ 4	5		+ 3	2
8	1			

```
  8 5 3        3 6        8 2 7        4 7 5
+   3 9      + 3 8 2    + 4 9 6      + 7 1 5
```

WHAT'S THE NUMBER?

A place-value table can help you understand whole numbers. Each digit in a number has a value based on its place in the number.

The 3 is in the millions place.
Its value is 3 millions, or 3,000,000.

The 8 is in the hundred thousands place.
Its value is 8 hundred thousands, or 800,000.

The 6 is in the tens place.
Its value is 6 tens, or 60.

hundred millions	ten millions	millions	hundred thousands	ten thousands	thousands	hundreds	tens	ones
3	8	0	2	5	6	7		

Now it's your turn! Write each number in the place value table.

1. 409
2. 61,023
3. 8,921,800
4. 647,369

hundred millions	ten millions	millions	hundred thousands	ten thousands	thousands	hundreds	tens	ones
1. | | | | | | | 4 | 0 | 9 |
2. | | | | | | | | | |
3. | | | | | | | | | |
4. | | | | | | | | | |

Write each number in the table. Then write the place name for the 2 in each number.

5. 361,250   hundreds
6. 2,035   _____
7. 592   _____
8. 24,837   _____

Write each number in the table. Then write the value of the underlined digit.

9. 6<u>3</u>,429   3 thousands
10. 17,60<u>1</u>   _____
11. 5<u>8</u>4   _____
12. <u>4</u>09,576   _____

PATTERNS ARE EVERYWHERE

Patterns are how things are ordered. You can solve some problems by looking for a pattern.

 Read the problem.

The picture shows the necklace Lashad is making. Lashad is using a pattern to make the necklace. How will the necklace look when she adds 3 more beads?

 Find the pattern and write the rule.

2 small dotted beads and 1 large striped bead.

 Solve the problem.

This is how the necklace will look after Lashad adds 3 more beads.

Now it's your turn! Find the pattern to solve the problem.

1. A new store has flags outside. Draw the shapes of the next 3 flags in the row.

2. Write the missing number:
   12, 22, 32, 42, _____, 62

3. Draw the item that goes next in the pattern.

4. Write the next two numbers:
   117, 119, 121, _____, _____

NUMBERS AND WORDS

Write each number in words.

1. An airplane can fly at 32,000 feet over sea level.

Thirty-two thousand _____

2. Pike's Peak, a mountain in Colorado, is 14,110 feet above sea level.

_____

_____

3. Denver, Colorado, is called the "Mile-high" City because it is 1 mile above sea level. There are 5,280 feet in a mile.

_____

_____

4. There are 86,400 seconds in a day.

_____

_____

5. The ostrich is the largest bird. It can weigh up to 344 pounds.

_____

_____

6. The Statue of Liberty is 302 feet high.

_____

_____

Write each number in digits.

7. The largest cloud, called cumulonimbus, can weigh up to one billion pounds.

_____

8. The Egyptian Sphinx is two hundred forty feet long.

_____

9. Jupiter measures almost eighty-nine thousand miles across.

_____

Write each number in digits and in words.

10. The number of people in your school:

_____

_____

11. The number of people in your class:

_____

_____

THE THREE "R"s

That's what Reading and 'Riting and 'Rithmetic were called in the "good old" days. We read and write the number in the place value chart as twenty-five thousand, three hundred seventy.

The digit 2 means 2 ten thousands, or 20,000.
The digit 5 means 5 thousands, or 5,000.
The digit 3 means 3 hundreds, or 300.
The digit 7 means 7 tens, or 70.
The digit 0 means 0 ones, or 0.

Notice that commas separate the digits into groups of three. This helps make larger numbers easier to read.

Now it's your turn! Rewrite each number. Insert commas where needed.

1.	289701	289,701	156823	_____	16208329	_____
2.	8067	_____	76170	_____	741038	_____
3.	9265081	_____	1972493	_____	928492	_____

Write each number in digits. Insert commas where needed.

4. Four hundred sixty thousand, nine hundred twelve 460,912

5. Three million, eighty-one thousand, fifty-six _____

6. Seventy thousand, one hundred thirty-nine _____

MATH MADNESS

1 Harriet the Handy Woman isn't very handy with place value. Every number is out of place, it seems to her. She is trying to build a place value chart for the number seven thousand, three hundred two, but something is wrong. Make a new place value chart to help Harriet.

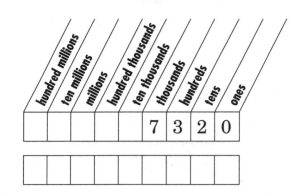

hundred millions	ten millions	millions	hundred thousands	ten thousands	thousands	hundreds	tens	ones
					7	3	2	0

2 Harriet can't figure out why this problem is wrong. You can switch two numbers in the ones place to correct this problem. Which numbers can you switch? Help Harriet correct this problem.

412 - 251 = 163

3 You have a number with 3 thousands, 9 hundreds, 5 tens, and 4 ones. Make a place value chart, and write the number. What place value changes if you take away 300? Write the new number in the chart below the old number.

hundred millions	ten millions	millions	hundred thousands	ten thousands	thousands	hundreds	tens	ones

Name _____ Date _____

MAMMA MIA! THAT'S A LOT OF PIZZAS!

Sometimes a problem has many facts. Putting the facts in a table can help you see how the facts go together. Then the problem is easier to solve.

 Read the problem.

Jack works in Pete's Peppy Pizza Parlor on weekends when they sell the most pizzas. On Saturday he sold 40 cheese pizzas, 32 sausage pizzas, and 55 pepperoni pizzas. On Sunday he sold 12 cheese pizzas, 24 sausage pizzas, and 37 pepperoni pizzas. A cheese pizza costs $2.00, a sausage pizza costs $4.00, and a pepperoni pizza costs $5.00. This weekend which kind of pizza did Jack sell the most?

STEP 2 **List the facts.**

Fact 1. *On Saturday Jack sold 40 cheese pizzas, 32 sausage pizzas, and 55 pepperoni pizzas. On Sunday Jack sold 12 cheese pizzas, 24 sausage pizzas, and 37 pepperoni pizzas.*

Fact 2. *A cheese pizza costs $2.00, a sausage pizza costs $4.00, and a pepperoni pizza costs $5.00*

STEP 3 **Make a table.**

Put all the facts into the table.

	Cheese Pizza $2.00	Sausage Pizza $4.00	Pepperoni Pizza $5.00
Saturday	40	32	55
Sunday	12	24	37
Totals			

 Solve the problem.

Add the number of each kind of pizza.

40	32	55
+12	+24	+37
52 cheese	56 sausage	92 pepperoni

Jack sold the most pepperoni pizzas.

Name _____ Date _____

MAMMA MIA! LOTS MORE PIZZAS!

	Cheese Pizza $2.00	Sausage Pizza $4.00	Pepperoni Pizza $5.00
Saturday	40	32	55
Sunday	12	24	37
Totals			

Now it's your turn! Fill in the table, then solve the problems.

1. How many sausage pizzas did Jack sell on both days? _____

2. On which day did Jack sell more pizzas? _____

3. Which pizza costs the most? _____

4. How much would it cost to
   buy one of each kind of pizza? _____

5. How many and what kinds of pizzas could you buy for $9.00?
   (HINT - There are 2 correct answers.)

   _____

   _____

6. You want to buy 2 cheese
   pizzas and 3 pepperoni
   pizzas for a party.
   How much will they cost?

   _____

SHEILA SELLS SEASHELLS BY THE SEA SHORE!

Some problems may give more facts than you need. Read the problem. Decide which facts you need and which are extra. Cross out the extra facts. Use the facts that are left to solve the problem.

STEP 1 **Read the problem.**
Sheila collects seashells at the beach. She sells them for $1.00 each. One week she found 34 shells. The next week she found 16 shells. How many shells did Sheila find during those 2 weeks?

STEP 2 **Decide which facts you need.**
Fact 1: *The first week she found 34 shells.*
Fact 2: *The next week she found 16 shells.*

STEP 3 **Decide which facts are extra.**
She sells them for $1.00 each.

STEP 4 **Solve the problem.**
34 + 16 = 50. Sheila found 50 shells in 2 weeks.

Now it's your turn! Cross out extra facts. Then solve the problem.

1. 14 girls and 18 boys went swimming. Each girl wore a red bathing suit. How many children went swimming?

   _____

2. Pedro plays beach volleyball. His team plays 20 games during a season. So far they have won 6 games and lost 3. How many games has the team played this season?

   _____

Name _____ Date _____

HOW MANY? ABOUT THAT MANY!

You do not always need an exact answer to solve a problem. You can solve such problems by estimating. To estimate, round each number to the same place. Then add the rounded numbers.

 Read the problem.
About how much is 64 + 37? (Remember, *about* means you do not need an exact answer.)

 Round each number to the nearest tens place.
64 → 60   37 → 40

 Add to solve the problem.
60 + 40 = 100

Now it's your turn! Round the numbers to the nearest tens place, then add.

1. Miss Garcia's class held a bake sale. They sold 66 cupcakes and 53 cookies. About how many cupcakes and cookies did they sell altogether?

   66 → _____   53 → _____
   _____

   What is your favorite kind of cookie? _____

2. The cafeteria serves 247 students in the first lunch period and 369 students in the second lunch period. About how many students are served in both lunch periods?

   247 → _____   369 → _____
   _____

   In which lunch period do they serve more? _____

3. 122 fathers and 96 mothers went to the school's open house. About how many parents went to the open house?

   122 → _____   96 → _____
   _____

Problem Solving 3-4, SV 6759-X

Name _____ Date _____

MOM! I DON'T HAVE ANYTHING TO WEAR!

Sometimes it helps to make a list to solve a problem. Put the information in order. Then it will be easy to see how to solve the problem.

 STEP 1 **Read the problem.**
Suzy has a red t-shirt and a green blouse. She also has blue jeans and black slacks. How many different combinations of clothing does she have?

 STEP 2 **Make a list.**
Start by listing the colors of her tops. Then list the colors of her pants. Draw lines between the lists to match each top with pants. Then write the matches.

Tops	Pants	Matches
red t-shirt → blue jeans green blouse → black slacks		red t-shirt - blue jeans red t-shirt - black slacks green blouse - blue jeans green blouse - black slacks

 STEP 3 **Solve the problem.**
Count the combinations. There are 4 different ways Suzy can mix her clothes.

Now it's your turn! Make a list to solve this problem.

1. A snack shop has white and whole wheat bread. It has tuna, ham, and turkey for sandwiches. How many different kinds of sandwiches can they make? _____

2. If one more kind of bread is added, how many different kinds of sandwiches can they make? _____

   Is there a pattern? _____

Name _____ Date _____

IT'S SNACK TIME. YUMMY!

 Read the problem.
Keisha's favorite snacks are blueberry muffins, oatmeal cookies, and yogurt. Her favorite drinks are milk and juice. How many different combinations of 1 snack and 1 drink can Keisha make?

 Make a list.

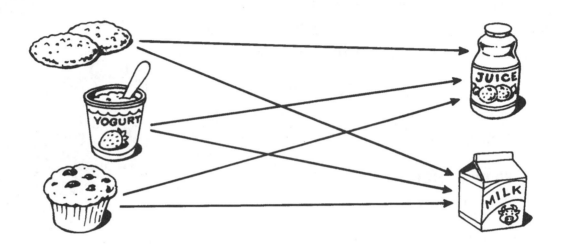

 Solve the problem.
Keisha can make 6 different snack combinations.

Now it's your turn! Make a list to solve these problems.

1. Samir has a terrier and a poodle. He has brown and white collars for the dogs. How many different ways can he use the collars for his dogs?

   _____

2. Kim wants to make a picture. She can use crayons, paints, or markers. She may make her pictures on white paper, yellow paper, or blue paper. How many different ways can she make a picture?

   _____

Name _____ Date _____

THERE'S SOMETHING FISHY AT THE AQUARIUM!

Sometimes a problem does not tell you whether to add or subtract. Read the problem carefully, and decide if you need to add or subtract. Then solve the problem.

 Read the Problem.

Julio's class went to the Aquarium on a field trip. In the first tank they saw 67 fish. In the next tank they saw 138 fish. How many fish did they see in both tanks?

 Decide what the problem is asking.

This problem asks, *"How many fish did they see in both tanks?"*

 Choose an operation.

Add to find how many fish.

 Solve the problem.

67 + 138 = 205. Julio's class saw 205 fish in both tanks.

Now it's your turn! Circle the operation. Solve the problem.

1. Cho counted the students in his school. There were 326 boys and 348 girls. How many students go to Cho's school? Add? Subtract?
_____
How does the number of the students in Cho's school compare to your school?
_____

2. A baker bought 540 pounds of sugar. He used 265 pounds to bake cakes. How much sugar is left? Add? Subtract?
_____

MATH MADNESS

THINK!

A single problem can contain many different problems.

1 The school bus makes four stops each day. At the first stop, 1 boy and 2 girls get on the bus. At the next stop, 2 boys and 3 girls get on. At the third stop, 3 boys and 4 girls get on. Do you see the pattern?

At the last stop before school, how many boys get on the bus? _____

How many girls get on at the last stop? _____

Altogether how many children get on the bus?
_____

2 At your school, 267 students ride the bus, 102 ride their bikes, and 68 ride with their parents. Another 32 students walk to school. About how many students go to your school? _____

3 Here's a tricky one. Mr. and Mrs. Abbott have 3 children, 2 boys and a girl. They would like to have 6 boys, and arrange it so each boy has a sister. How many more girls do they have to have for this to happen? _____

HEY! HEY! VOTE FOR SHAY! NO! NO! VOTE FOR BO!

Sometimes a problem has many facts. Putting the facts in a table can help you see how the facts go together. Then the problem is easier to solve.

Washington Elementary held an election for student council. Complete the table to show the election results.

Fill in the table with these facts:

1. Shay Wilson got 49 votes from the 3rd grade, 39 votes from the 4th grade, and 61 votes from the 5th grade.

2. Bo Rodriquez got 14 votes from the 3rd grade, 57 votes from the 4th grade, and 55 votes from the 5th grade.

number of votes

	3rd grade	4th grade	5th grade	total
Shay				
Bo				

Now it's your turn! Use the table to solve these problems.

1. How many more 3rd graders voted for Shay than for Bo? _____

2. How many more votes did Bo get from the 4th grade than from the 3rd grade? _____

3. Who got more total votes from the 4th and 5th grades? _____

4. How many more votes did the winner get than the loser? _____

5. Who won the election? _____

TO THE LIBRARY!

Sometimes a problem does not tell you whether to add or subtract. Decide what the problem is asking. Do you add or subtract? Choose the right operation to solve the problem.

STEP 1 **Read the problem.**
Your school library has 530 CD ROM titles and 421 filmstrip titles. How many more CD ROM titles are there?

add?
```
  530
+ 421
-----
  951
```

STEP 2 **Circle the correct operation.**
To find out how many more, you must subtract.

subtract?
```
  530
- 421
-----
  109
```

STEP 3 **Solve the problem.**
530 - 421 = 109. There are 109 more CD ROM titles than filmstrip titles.

Now it's your turn! Choose the correct operation. Solve the problem.

1. Tia has a book with 204 pages. There are pictures on 28 pages. How many pages do not have pictures?

add?
```
  204
+  28
```

subtract?
```
  204
-  28
```

2. Raul read for 92 minutes on Monday and 49 minutes on Tuesday. How much longer did he read on Monday than on Tuesday?

add?
```
  92
+ 49
```

subtract?
```
  92
- 49
```

IF YOU CAN'T USE IT, CUT IT OUT!

Some problems may give more facts than you need. Read the problem. Decide which facts you need and which are extra. Cross out the extra facts. Use the facts that are left to solve the problem.

STEP 1 **Read the problem.**
Patti has saved $153 to buy a new basketball hoop and net. One brand costs $96. Another brand costs $105. What is the difference in the cost between the 2 brands?

STEP 2 **Decide which facts are needed.**
Fact 1: *One brand costs $96.*
Fact 2: *The other brand costs $105.*

STEP 3 **Decide which facts are extra.**
Patti has saved $153.

STEP 4 **Solve the problem.**
$105 - $96 = $9.
One brand costs $9 more than the other.

Now it's your turn! Cross out extra information to solve each problem.

1. When the Garza family went to the Superbowl, they drove 741 miles in 2 days. Mr. Garza drove 50 miles per hour all the way. The first day he drove 447 miles. How many miles did he drive the second day?

   _____

2. Juan collects sports trading cards. He has 172 baseball cards, 199 football cards, and 88 basketball cards. How many more baseball cards than basketball cards does he have? _____

EE! EYE! EE! EYE! YO!

You do not always need an exact answer to solve a problem. You can solve some problems by estimating. To estimate, round each number to the same place. Then subtract the rounded numbers.

Old MacDonald raises cows on his farm. In April his cows produced 1,316 gallons of milk. He sold 918 gallons of milk. About how many gallons were left?

 Estimate to the nearest hundred.
1,316 → 1,300   918 → 900

 Solve the problem.
1,300 - 900 = 400
About 400 gallons were left.

Now it's your turn! Round to the nearest hundred, then solve.

1. Old MacDonald drove 6,322 miles in his green pick-up truck. He drove 4,588 miles in his blue car. About how many more miles did he drive in his truck than in his car? _____

2. Termites ate Old MacDonald's fence posts! He must replace them. (The posts, not the termites.) He bought 2,305 fence posts. He replaced 917 posts. About how many fence posts are left to replace? _____

3. On his farm (really, it's a ranch), he had 12,642 head of cattle. He took 11,011 on a cattle drive. About how many head of cattle remained on the ranch? _____

4. Of the 26,341 acres of land on his ranch, he has cattle on 24,679 acres. About how many acres do not have cattle on them? _____

Name _____ Date _____

WHAT A SPORT!

Students at your school voted for their favorite sports. The bar graph shows the number of votes each sport received.

To read a bar graph, line up the top of each bar with the number on the left.

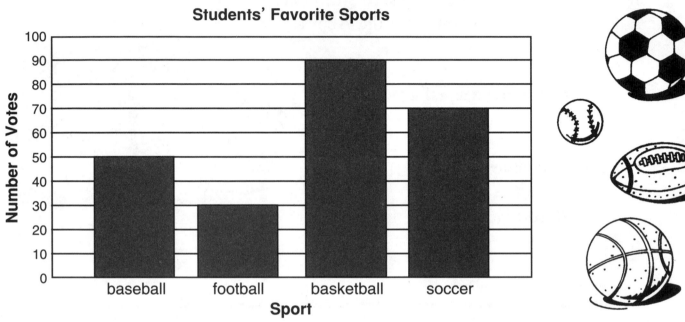

Now it's your turn! Use the graph to solve the problems.

1. What is the favorite sport? _____

2. How many more votes did the favorite
sport receive than the next favorite? _____

3. Each student had 1 vote.
About how many students voted? _____

4. How many more students voted
for soccer than for football? _____

REUBEN IS A SLUGGER!

Sometimes it helps to start at the end of a problem and work backwards.

 STEP 1 **Read the problem.**
Reuben has scored 142 runs for his team so far this year. He scored 12 runs yesterday. How many runs did he score before yesterday?

 STEP 2 **List the facts.**
Fact 1: *Reuben scored 142 runs.*
Fact 2: *He scored 12 runs yesterday.*

STEP 3 **Solve the problem.**
142 - 12 = 130. Reuben scored 130 runs before yesterday.

Now it's your turn! Work backwards to solve these problems.

1. Shari gave out 59 programs before the game started. By the time the game ended, she had given out 217 programs. How many programs did she give out during the game? _____

2. Valencia sold 48 bags of peanuts at the ball game. She has 76 more bags to sell. How many bags of peanuts did she have when she started selling?
_____

3. If Valencia earned about $96 selling peanuts at the ball game (Question #2), how much was each bag? _____

4. After Valencia has sold all of the bags of peanuts, will she have $200? _____

How much more or less than $200 will she have? _____

Name _____ Date _____

FOR THE BIRDS!

Sometimes a problem has more than 1 part.

 Read the problem.

Allegra has a birdhouse in her backyard. In June she saw 57 birds visit the birdhouse. She saw 16 fewer birds in May. How many birds visited the house in both months?

 Solve the first part.

Find the number of birds she saw in May.

$57 - 16 = 41$

STEP 3 **Solve the second part.**

Find the number of birds she saw in both months.

$57 + 41 = 98$

Now it's your turn! Use a two-part plan to solve these problems.

1. Pablo bought binoculars for $7.00 and a book on birds for $5.00. He gave the clerk $15.00. How much change did he get back? _____

2. Rosa photographed 144 birds. There were 62 cardinals and 54 sparrows. The rest of the birds were robins. How many robins did Rosa photograph?

_____

3. Rosa bought 50 lbs. of bird feed. She used 17 lbs. the first week and 15 lbs. the second week. How much does she have for next week?

_____

4. Pablo bought supplies for $213. He used $75 for bird feed and $15 for sugar. If he spent the rest of the money for bird feeders, how much did he spend for bird feeders?

_____

1 30 days have September, April, June, and November. All the rest have 31, except poor February, with only 28. But in a leap year, it has 29 days! How many months have 28 days?_____(Be careful, and think ahead!)

2 Ugh and Duh are cavemen. They use sticks for numbers. A single stick stands for 1; 2 sticks stand for 2; and so on. Ugh has a lot of trouble learning how to add and subtract. One day, he asks Duh for help with his homework. Ugh has placed 11 sticks like this:

"Something is wrong," says Duh.
"The sticks read 2 - 4 = 2."

You can solve the problem by moving just 1 stick. Sure you can. You're smarter than a caveman! Which stick do you move? Draw your answer in the box.

SATURDAY NIGHT AT THE MOVIES

Some problems do not tell you whether to add, subtract, multiply, or divide. Read the problem carefully. Decide what the problem is asking you to do. Choose an operation, then solve the problem.

STEP 1 ▷ **Read the problem.**

Erica has 3 boxes of microwave popcorn to share while watching movies with friends. Each box has 4 bags of popcorn inside. If each of her friends eats 1 bag, will Erica have enough popcorn for 10 people?

STEP 2 ▷ **Decide what the problem is asking.**

"How many bags of popcorn does she have altogether?"
Find a sum or product.

STEP 3 ▷ **Choose an operation.**

To solve the problem, you can add 4 three times. With equal parts it is faster to multiply 4 x 3.

STEP 4 ▷ **Solve the problem.**

4 + 4 + 4 = 12   *OR*   4 x 3 = 12
Erica has enough popcorn!

Now it's your turn! Choose the correct operation, then solve.

1. Adrienne has 2 empty shelves in her bookcase. Each shelf holds 28 videos. How many videos can she put on the shelves? _____
   Circle the correct operation.

   $$\begin{array}{r} 2\,8 \\ \times\ \ 2 \\ \hline \end{array} \qquad 2\overline{)2\,8}$$

   Does she have room for 50 videos? _____

2. Mr. Watts works 9 hours a day at the theater. He works 6 days a week. How many hours does he work each week? _____

   The average work week is 40 hours. How much more does Mr. Watts work?

   _____

Name _____   Date _____

HOORAY!! THE CIRCUS IS COMING TO TOWN!

You do not always need an exact answer to solve a problem. Some problems can be solved by estimating. Round each number to the same place. Then multiply the rounded numbers.

STEP 1 > **Read the problem.**
Shontal sold 17 t-shirts at the circus for $8 each. Her goal was to sell $100 worth of t-shirts. Did she reach her goal?

STEP 2 > **Identify the important facts.**
Shontal sold 17 t-shirts. They cost $8 each.
She wanted to sell $100 in t-shirts.

STEP 3 > **Round all numbers.**
17 → 20 $8 → $10

STEP 4 > **Solve the problem.**
20 x $10 = $200
$200 is more than $100. Shontal met her goal.

Now it's your turn! Use estimation to solve these problems.

1. There are 12 dogs in the show. Each dog is 19 inches long. If the dogs are put end to end, about how many inches long would they be in all? _____

   How many feet is that?

   _____

2. The school band wants to wear gold-braided hats for the circus parade. The band has $480. Is there enough money to buy fancy hats for 46 students if each hat costs $13? _____

3. If the fierce lion sleeps 16 hours a day, about how many hours will it sleep in 10 days?

   _____

4. Nick, the elephant keeper, had 8 bushels of apples. There were 38 apples in a bushel. Nick gave 4 bushels of apples to Sue, who made taffy apples. About how many apples were left to feed the elephant?

   _____

Name _____ Date _____

PIZZA, PIZZA!!
WHO'S GOT THE PIZZA?

Sometimes a problem has many facts. Organizing the facts in a table helps show how the facts go together. You can use the table to solve the problem.

 STEP 1 **Read the problem.**

Jack's Pizza Shop is doing well. On Saturday he sold 40 cheese pizzas, 32 sausage pizzas, and 55 pepperoni pizzas. Cheese pizzas cost $2.00 each, sausage pizzas cost $4.00 each, and pepperoni pizzas cost $5.00 each. How much money did Jack take in on Saturday?

 STEP 2 **List the facts.**

Fact 1: *On Saturday he sold 40 cheese pizzas, 32 sausage pizzas, and 55 pepperoni pizzas.*

Fact 2: *Cheese pizzas cost $2.00, sausage pizzas cost $4.00, and pepperoni pizzas cost $5.00.*

 STEP 3 **Make a table.**

	Cheese	Sausage	Pepperoni
Saturday sales	40	32	55
Cheese $2	$2 x 40 = A		
Sausage $4		$4 x 32 = B	
Pepperoni $5			$5 x 55 = C
Totals	**A**	**B**	**C**

 STEP 4 **Solve the problem.**

Add together the totals.   A + B + C = ?

Now it's your turn! Use the table to solve the problem.

1. How much money did Jack take in on Saturday? _____

2. On which kind of pizza did he take in the most money? _____

GO ON TO NEXT PAGE

Name _____ Date _____

PIZZA, PIZZA!!
WHO'S GOT THE PIZZA? PART 2

Now it's your turn! Complete this table to solve Problem 1.

	Cheese	Sausage	Pepperoni
Sunday sales	12	24	37
Cheese $2	$2 x ? = A		
Sausage $4		$4 x ? = B	
Pepperoni $5			$5 x ? = C
Totals	**A**	**B**	**C**

1. On Sunday, Jack sold 12 cheese pizzas, 24 sausage pizzas, and 37 pepperoni pizzas. How much money did Jack take in on Sunday?

   _____

   Did he take in more on Saturday or Sunday? _____
   Which pizza brought in the most money for the 2 days? _____

Make your own tables to solve these problems.

2. Jack used 6 tomatoes, 3 onions, and 12 cups of shredded cheese to make pizzas. He made 3 pizzas. How much of each ingredient did he use for each pizza?

   _____

   _____

   _____

   What else do you think he should put on the pizzas?

   _____

   _____

3. Jack wants to buy in-line skates with the money he earns selling pizza. He earns $5.00 an hour. On Friday he worked 6 hours. On Saturday he worked 8 hours. On Sunday he worked 7 hours. How much money did Jack earn this weekend?

   _____

Name _____ Date _____

"RAH, RAH, RAH! GO TEAM!"

Some problems can be solved by finding a pattern. Read the problem carefully. Look for a pattern. Write the rule that makes and completes the pattern. Then solve the problem.

 STEP 1 **Read the problem.**
What are the next two numbers in this pattern?
3, 9, 27, . . .

 STEP 2 **Determine the relationship.**
⌐x3⌐ ⌐x3⌐
3,   9,   27, . . .

 STEP 3 **Write the rule.**
Multiply by 3.

STEP 4 **Solve the problem.**
27 x 3 = 81   81 x 3 = 243
The next two numbers are 81 and 243.

Now it's your turn! Find a pattern to solve these problems.

1. Tiffany's teammates have jerseys numbered 20, 25, and 35. Tiffany's jersey is missing. What is her number? Number the jerseys below.

Fill in the blanks with the next 2 numbers in each sequence.

2. 2, 5, 8, 11, _____, _____

3. 198, 297, 396 , _____, _____

4. 60, 63, 58, 61, _____, _____

5. 42, 49, 56, _____, _____

"PLAY BALL!"

When given the outcome, work backwards to solve the problem. Read carefully to find clues. Then work backwards.

STEP 1 ▷ **Read the problem.**

Mrs. Perez gave her 5 basketball players the same number of warm-up exercises. After Janelle did 2 exercises, she had 7 left to finish. Altogether how many warm-up exercises did the team do?

STEP 2 ▷ **List the clues.**

Clue A: There are 5 basketball team players.
Clue B: They all have the same number of warm-up exercises.
Clue C: Janelle has already done 2 warm-up exercises.
Clue D: She has 7 warm-up exercises left to finish.

STEP 3 ▷ **Work backwards.**

Start at the end of the problem.
- Add the number of exercises Janelle has left to the exercises she has done. $7 + 2 = 9$
- Multiply the number of Janelle's warm-up exercises by the number of players. $9 \times 5 = 45$

STEP 4 ▷ **Solve the problem.**

Altogether the team did 45 exercises.

Now it's your turn! Work backwards to solve the problems.

1. The golf coach gave 6 players the same number of golf balls. After Tim hit 4 golf balls, he had 3 left. How many golf balls in all did the coach give the players? _____

   If he gives the players the same number of balls every day, how long will 200 golf balls last?

   _____

2. Johnny has 30 pages left to read in his sports almanac. Yesterday he read twice that many pages. The first day he read 5 more pages than yesterday. How many pages are in his almanac? _____

   In what other books might he look for similar information?

   _____

Name _____ Date _____

SHOWING SCHOOL SPIRIT

Sometimes it helps to make a list to solve a multiplication problem. When you put the information in a list in an organized way, it is easy to see how to solve the problem.

 Read the Problem.

Thorp School sells shirts, pants, and shorts. Each comes in school colors, blue or gold. How many combinations of outfits are there?

 Make a list.

List each color of sweatshirt in the left column. Write each color of pants in the next column. Draw lines to match each shirt with each pair of pants. Write the matches.

Sweatshirts Pants	Matches
blue shirt → blue pants, gold pants, blue shorts, gold shorts gold shirt → blue pants, gold pants, blue shorts, gold shorts	blue shirt/blue pants blue shirt/gold pants blue shirt/blue shorts blue shirt/gold shorts gold shirt/blue pants gold shirt/gold pants gold shirt/blue shorts gold shirt/gold shorts

 Solve the problem.

Count the different matches.
Shortcut! Multiply:

```
  2  kinds of shirts
x 4  kinds of pants
  8  different matches
```

Now it's your turn! Make a list or multiply to solve.

1. Paige has pink, blue, and black leotards. She has white and pink ballet slippers. How many different combinations of leotards and slippers can she wear? _____

MATH MADNESS

1 Poor Harriet. She is having a very difficult time with her multiplication. Please help Harriet find the product of these numbers. You can do it!

(Hint: Look at the whole problem before you start multiplying.)

27 x 4 x 567 x 18 x 55 x 943 x 0 = _____

2 This multiplication problem gives the answer. You will have to figure out the problem! A, B, and C are single digit numbers that you have to find. There is more than one way to do this. Try and see!

$$A + (B \times C) = 27$$

A = _____   B = _____   C = _____

3 Pablo and Carlos are riding their bikes on a flat road that is 20 miles long. They start at opposite ends and ride toward each other at a speed of 10 miles per hour. A bee flies back and forth from Carlos' bike to Pablo's at 15 miles per hour until they meet in the middle. How far will the bee have flown when they meet? _____ (Hint: Think about how much time it takes the bee to fly.)

4 Do you know what a dozen is? A dozen is 12 of anything. A dozen eggs is 12 eggs. A dozen widgets is 12 widgets. If there are 12 one-cent stamps in a dozen, how many two-cent stamps are in a dozen? _____

Name _____ Date _____

YANKEE DOODLE COMES TO TOWN!

Sometimes a problem does not tell you whether to add, subtract, multiply, or divide. Read the problem carefully, and decide what the problem is asking you to do. Choose an operation, then solve the problem.

STEP 1 **Read the problem.**

Mr. Johnson has 36 American flags in 6 boxes. If each box holds the same number of flags, how many flags are in each box?

STEP 2 **Decide what the problem is asking.**

In this problem, the question "how many . . . in each" is asking you to find equal parts.

STEP 3 **Choose an operation.**

To solve this problem, you must divide.

STEP 4 **Solve the problem.**

36 ÷ 6 = 6. There are 6 American flags in each box.

Now it's your turn! Choose the correct operation to solve these problems.

1. Mr. Wojak is cutting watermelon at the 4th of July picnic. He serves 12 people from each watermelon. If there are 60 people at the picnic, how many watermelons will he need?

   _____

2. There are 24 children at the picnic. Each child gets 6 sparklers. If there are 6 sparklers in a box, how many boxes do they use?

   _____

   If there are 12 boxes in a case, how many cases do they use? _____

Name _____ Date _____

OLYMPICS, HERE WE COME!

When given the outcome, work backwards to solve the problem. Read carefully to find the clues. Then work backwards.

 Read the problem.
Danielle, Genie, and Zoe take gymnastics. Danielle can do 4 more cartwheels than Genie. Genie can do half as many cartwheels as Zoe. Zoe does 8 cartwheels. How many cartwheels does Danielle do?

List the clues.
 Clue 1: *Danielle can do 4 more cartwheels than Genie.*
Clue 2: *Genie can do half as many cartwheels as Zoe.*
Clue 3: *Zoe does 8 cartwheels.*

 Solve the problem.
Start at the end of the project and work backwards.
* *Genie can do half as many cartwheels as Zoe.* $8 \div 2 = 4$
  Genie does 4 cartwheels.
* *Danielle can do 4 more cartwheels than Genie.* $4 + 4 = 8$
  Danielle does 8 cartwheels.

Now it's your turn! Work backwards to solve these problems.

1. Raul knows 2 wrestling holds less than Jeff does. Jeff knows 3 more than Ian. Ian knows 9 holds. How many wrestling holds does Raul know?

   _____

   Who knows the most wrestling holds? _____

2. Today Alfred swam 30 practice laps in the pool. Yesterday he swam 10 laps less than today. Tomorrow he will swim 10 more than today. How many practice laps will Alfred have done in the 3 days? _____

Name _____ Date _____

AS EASY AS PIE!

The answer to a problem may be found by recognizing a pattern. Read the problem carefully. Look for a pattern. Then write the rule that makes and completes the pattern. Solve the problem.

 Read the problem.

Mark made pies for a bake sale. He made 96 pies the first week, 48 pies the next week, 24 pies the 3rd week, and 12 pies the 4th week. How many pies did he make the 5th week and 6th week?

 Determine the relationship.

$$\overset{\div 2}{96,} \quad \overset{\div 2}{48,} \quad \overset{\div 2}{24,} \quad 12, \ldots$$

 Write the rule.

Divide by 2.

 Solve the problem.

$12 \div 2 = 6 \quad 6 \div 2 = 3$

Mark made 6 pies the 5th week, and 3 pies the 6th week.

Now it's your turn! Find a pattern to solve these problems.

1. The Smith's Ice Cream Shop is celebrating their 3rd anniversary with a special give-away. Each time someone orders a scoop of ice cream, Mr. Smith gives away free toppings! LaNelle ordered 9 scoops and received 3 free toppings. Willy ordered 6 scoops and received 2 free toppings. If Emil orders 12 scoops of ice cream, how many free toppings will he get?

_____

2. To celebrate the anniversary, the Smiths sponsor a race. Their daughter Sandra is Runner C. Runner A is number 256, Runner B is number 64, and Runner D is number 4. What is Sandra's number?

_____

3. The first place winner in the marathon gets $250; second gets $50; third gets $10. How much does the fourth place runner get?_____

WE HAVE A MYSTERY TO SOLVE!

3. Cory received this secret message from his friend Jerry. Can you decode the message? Write the letter under each problem with the matching answer.

A	B	C	E	F	H	I	M	O	R	T	W
18	3	15	4	42	21	6	13	9	5	12	0

__ __ __ __ __ __   __ __ __   __ __ __

   First Word   **Second Word**   **Third Word**

$27 \div 9 =$ ___ $45 \div 5 =$ ___ $72 \div 6 =$ ___

$16 \div 4 =$ ___ $126 \div 3 =$ ___ $105 \div 5 =$ ___

$13 \div 0 =$ ___ $64 \div 16 =$ ___

$36 \div 2 =$ ___

$125 \div 25 =$ ___

$48 \div 12 =$ ___

__ __ __ __ __   __ __ __ __

   Fourth Word   **Fifth Word**

$143 \div 11 =$ ___ $63 \div 3 =$ ___

$234 \div 13 =$ ___ $54 \div 3 =$ ___

$145 \div 29 =$ ___ $40 \div 8 =$ ___

$75 \div 5 =$ ___ $92 \div 23 =$ ___

$441 \div 21 =$ ___

The secret message says:

_____

Name _____ Date _____

APRIL SHOWERS BRING MAY FLOWERS

A graph is a special table of facts. In a picture graph, pictures stand for facts. A bar graph contains information in the shape of bars.

STEP 1 **Read the problem.**

The florist keeps track of how many roses she ordered. How many more roses did she order in May, compared to June and to October?

STEP 2 **Read the graph.**

A. Find the labels for May, June, and October at the bottom of the graph.

B. Move your finger to the top of the bar for each of those months. Then move across to the left to find the number of roses she ordered.

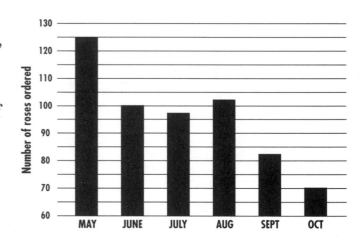

STEP 3 **Write the facts.**

Fact 1: In May she ordered 125 roses.

Fact 2: In June she ordered 100 roses.

Fact 3: In October she ordered 70 roses.

STEP 4 **Solve the problem.**

Subtract to find, "How many more?"

125 - 100 = 25   In May she ordered 25 more roses than in June.

125 - 70 = 55   In May she ordered 55 more roses than in October.

GO ON TO
NEXT PAGE

GOING TO THE THEATER

Sometimes you need to gather information before making a bar graph.

Now it's your turn! Use division to find out how many chairs are in each row. Then use the information to make your bar graph.

Mrs. Wilfong arranges chairs differently for each night of Summer Theater. A wide row with many chairs makes more stage space. A narrow row with few chairs makes more aisle space. The gymnastics show needs the most stage space. The comedy act needs the most aisle space.

Last week Mrs. Wilfong used 30 chairs. On Monday she made 2 rows, on Tuesday she made 3 rows, on Wednesday she made 5 rows, on Thursday she made 6 rows, and on Friday she made 10 rows.

1. How many chairs were in each row on . . .

Monday? _____   Tuesday? _____   Wednesday? _____

Thursday? _____   Friday? _____

2. Which night had the rows with the most chairs?

_____

3. Which night had the rows with the fewest chairs?

_____

4. The gymnastics show was on which night? _____

5. The comedy act was on which night? _____

Name _____ Date _____

FUNDRAISING IS FUN!

Often you do not need an exact answer to solve a problem. You can estimate the answer by rounding each number to the same place. Then divide to solve the problem.

 Read the problem.
To raise money for the school field trip, Noriko made $104 washing cars. She washed 19 cars. About how much did each person spend on a car wash?

Identify the important facts.
 Fact 1: *Noriko made $104 washing cars.*
Fact 2: *She washed 19 cars.*

 Round each number.
$104 → $100   19 → 20

 Solve the problem.
$100 ÷ 20 = $5
Each person spent about $5 for a car wash.

Now it's your turn! Use estimation to solve these problems.

1. Ramon sold 32 necklaces. He made $61. About how much did he make for each necklace? _____

2. Altogether, about how many necklaces will Ramon have to sell to pay for his $100 field trip? _____

3. Jessye sold 12 hair ribbons at a craft fair to raise money for her field trip. She made $64. About how much did each hair ribbon cost? _____

4. If Jessye still needs $36, about how many more hair ribbons must she sell?

   _____

MATH MADNESS

1 Harriet has 6 apples and there are 7 people at her house. She wants to share the apples equally. How can she do this? (This is a pretty sneaky way of dividing stuff!) _____

2 The lights went out at Harriet's house! She had to find her socks and shoes in total darkness. In her dresser drawer, she had a dozen loose black socks and 12 loose white socks. What is the smallest number of socks she could take out of the drawer to be sure she held a matching pair?

_____

3 The Sunshine Express train goes from New York City to Miami. The Big Town Limited goes from Miami to New York City on the same track. The Sunshine Express travels at 90 miles per hour, and the Big Town Limited travels at 60 miles per hour. If they leave at the same time, which train is closer to New York City when they meet? _____

STOCKING UP ON SCHOOL SUPPLIES

Some problems do not tell you whether to add, subtract, multiply, or divide. Read the problem carefully. Decide what the problem is asking you to do. Then solve the problem.

STEP 1 > **Read the problem.**
Jason has 4 boxes of striped pencils. There are 18 pencils in each box. How many pencils does Jason have?

STEP 2 > **Decide what the problem is asking.**
This problem asks, *"How many . . . altogether?"*

STEP 3 > **Choose an operation.**
Find a sum or product. To solve the problem, you could add 18 four times. Since there are equal parts, it is faster to multiply 4 x 18.

STEP 4 > **Solve the problem.**
18 + 18 + 18 + 18 = 72   *OR*   18 x 4 = 72
Jason has 72 pencils.

OR

STEP 1 > **Read the problem.**
Mrs. Kutsuwa
has 42 folders for
her students. Each student needs 2 folders. How many students does she have?

STEP 2 > **Decide what the problem is asking.**
This problem asks, *"How many students does she have?"* You must find equal parts.

STEP 3 > **Choose an operation.**
To solve, you must divide.

STEP 4 > **Solve the problem.**
42 ÷ 2 = 21   Mrs. Kutsuwa has 21 students.

Name _____ Date _____

STOCKING UP ON SCHOOL SUPPLIES, PART 2

Some problems do not tell you whether to add, subtract, multiply, or divide. Read the problem carefully. Decide what the problem is asking you to do. Then solve the problem.

Now it's your turn! Choose the correct operation, then solve these problems.

1. There are 13 cans of blue paint, 9 cans of red paint, and 11 cans of green paint on a shelf. How many cans of paint are on the shelf? _____

2. There are 5 test tubes in a box. The science class needs 45 test tubes for an experiment. How many boxes do they need? _____

3. The librarian counted 98 biographies in the school library. For their book reports, 26 students each checked out a biography. How many biographies were left? _____

4. There are 8 map colors in a box. Each student needs 4 colors for a map. If there are 36 students in the class, how many boxes of map colors does the class need? _____

5. Mr. Price has to pack a total of 48 calculators in the 4th grade math kits. He will make 8 kits. How many calculators will he put in each kit?

_____

6. D'Shawn has 32 beakers. She fills 17 beakers with water. How many beakers are left for her to fill? _____

SUMMER COOKING CLASS

A number sentence shows how numbers are related to each other. Read the problem, and find the clues. Write a number sentence. To solve the problem, you may need to work backwards.

 Read the problem.

Niljia used 3 teaspoons of water in her recipe. She also used some milk. Altogether she used 7 teaspoons of liquid. How much milk did she use?

 List the clues.

Clue 1: *Niljia used 3 teaspoons of water.*
Clue 2: *She also used some milk.*
Clue 3: *Altogether she used 7 teaspoons of liquid.*

 Write a number sentence.

teaspoons of milk + teaspoons of water = total teaspoons of liquid
  ?   +   3   =   7

 Solve the problem.

To find the missing number, work backwards.

? = 7 - 3   Since 7 - 3 = 4, Niljia used 4 teaspoons of milk.

Now it's your turn! Write number sentences to solve these problems.

1. Mr. Molina bought cookbooks for his students. He got 32 cookbooks. If each cooking class has 8 students, how many classes does Mr. Molina teach?_____

   If each class lasts for 13 weeks, how many groups of students does he have in a year?

   _____

2. Darlene has grilled 9 hotdogs at her summer party. Altogether she has to grill 16 hotdogs. How many more does she have to grill? _____

   If there are 8 hotdogs in each package, how many packages will she need? _____

A DAY AT THE RINK

When given the outcome, start at the end of the problem. Read the problem carefully, and find the clues. Then work backwards to solve the problem.

STEP 1 ▷ **Read the problem.**

Hal did 8 spins during ice skating practice. Scott did half as many spins as Hal. Ricardo did 2 more spins than Scott. How many spins each did Scott and Ricardo do?

STEP 2 ▷ **List the clues.**

Clue 1: *Hal did 8 spins.*
Clue 2: *Scott did half as many spins as Hal.*
Clue 3: *Ricardo did 2 more spins than Scott.*

STEP 3 ▷ **Solve the problem.**

Start at the end of the problem and work backwards.
Scott did half as many spins as Hal. $8 \div 2 = 4$ Scott did 4 spins.
Ricardo did 2 more spins than Scott. $4 + 2 = 6$ Ricardo did 6 spins.

Now it's your turn! Work backwards to solve these problems.

1. On Saturday morning Monique had $20 before going to the ice rink. She spent $6.00 for her lesson, $1.50 for skate rental, and 50¢ for a soda while she was there. She had $7 when she came home. How much had she spent before going to the ice rink?

   _____

2. Jenny won a jar of jelly beans in a skating contest. If you subtract 68 from the total number of jelly beans in the jar, the answer is 721. How many jelly beans are in Jenny's jar? _____
   How could you estimate the number of jelly beans in the jar? _____

   _____

ROY THE WRANGLER

Sometimes a problem has many facts. Organizing the facts in a table helps show how the facts go together. Use the table to solve the problem.

STEP 1 ➤ **Read the problem.**

Rowdy Roy works on a ranch. On Monday he ropes 6 horses, 9 sheep, and 7 steers. On Wednesday he ropes 8 horses, 10 sheep, and 13 steers. On Friday Roy ropes 4 horses, 12 sheep, and 18 steers. How many more animals does Roy rope on Friday than on Monday?

 STEP 2 ➤ **List the facts.**

Fact 1: *On Monday Roy ropes 6 horses, 9 sheep, and 7 steers.*
Fact 2: *On Wednesday Roy ropes 8 horses, 10 sheep, and 13 steers.*
Fact 3: *On Friday Roy ropes 4 horses, 12 sheep, and 18 steers.*

STEP 3 ➤ **Make a table.**

	Monday	Wednesday	Friday
horses	6	8	4
sheep	9	10	12
steers	7	13	18
Totals	**A**	**B**	**C**

 STEP 4 ➤ **Solve the problem.**

Add the numbers in the columns, then subtract.

$6 + 9 + 7 = 22$ $4 + 12 + 18 = 34$ $C - A = 12$

Roy ropes 12 more animals on Friday than he does on Monday.

Now it's your turn! Use the table above to solve these problems.

1. How many animals does Roy rope on Wednesday? _____

2. How many horses does Roy rope altogether? _____

   How many sheep in all? _____ How many steers in all? _____

DINOSAUR DILEMMAS

A way to solve some problems is to guess the answer, then check it. If it is not right, try again. Use what you learned from the first try to make your next guess better. Guess and check until you find the right answer.

STEP 1 **Read the problem.**

NaSha has a total of 10 plastic dinosaurs. She has 6 more green dinosaurs than brown ones. How many of each does she have?

STEP 2 **List the facts.**

NaSha has 10 plastic dinosaurs.
She has more green dinosaurs than brown ones.
She has at least 6 green plastic dinosaurs.

STEP 3 **Think about what numbers would give you the answer.**

Make a table of your guesses.
Guess 1: $6 + 4 = 10$ Check: $6 - 4 = 2$.   6 is only 2 more than 4.
Guess 2: $8 + 2 = 10$ Check: $8 - 2 = 6$.   8 is 6 more than 2.

NaSha has 8 green and 2 brown plastic dinosaurs.

Now it's your turn! Use Guess and Check to solve these problems.

1. Austin's friends made a dinosaur banner for his birthday party. The banner's perimeter is 32 feet. The long sides are 4 feet longer than the short sides. How long is each short side? _____

2. Jose and 7 friends are playing a dinosaur board game. The game has 19 cards. All players have a Brontosaurus card and a Triceratops card. Some players have a Tyrannosaurus Rex card. If all of the cards are being used, how many players have a Tyrannosaurus Rex card? _____

Name _____ Date _____

STARGAZING

You do not always need an exact answer to solve a problem. You can solve such problems by estimating. To estimate, round each number to the same place. Then choose an operation to solve the problem.

STEP 1 **Read the problem.**
Dale watched a movie and went to the observatory at an astronomy museum. The movie lasted 23 minutes. He was in the observatory for 47 minutes. For about how long was Dale at the museum?

STEP 2 **List the facts.**
Fact 1: *The movie lasted 23 minutes.*
Fact 2: *He was in the observatory for 47 minutes.*

STEP 3 **Round each number.**
23 → 20   47 → 50

STEP 4 **Solve the problem.**
20 + 50 = 70
Dale spent about 70 minutes at the museum.

Now it's your turn! Use estimation to solve these problems.

1. Alex counted 17 stars in an imaginary square in the sky. She estimated that she could see 24 squares in the sky, each with 17 stars. About how many stars could Alex see?

   _____

   When would Alex use this strategy?_____

   _____

   _____

2. Mario counted about 754 stars in the sky. If he filled the sky with 24 imaginary squares all the same size, about how many stars could he see in 1 square?

   _____

3. Keiko loves to read about the stars. If she read a total of 277 pages in 4 books, about how many pages are in each book?

   _____

MATH MADNESS

1 Harriet went to a dog show. In the ring she counted 22 heads and 72 feet. How many people and how many dogs were in the ring?
people _____   dogs _____

2 Harriet is working a word puzzle. Can you help her guess the missing word?

TAP ➡ PAL ➡ PAT ➡ ___ ___ ___

3 Harriet went camping by a river. She needed exactly 9 gallons of water to wash dishes. She had a 6-gallon bucket and a 5-gallon bucket. Using these she measured exactly 9 gallons.
How did she do it? (Hint: it helps to draw pictures of the buckets)

4 Harriet has been tossing a penny in the air and watching it come down heads or tails. The penny has rolled heads up 50 times in a row. What are the chances of the penny rolling heads up the next time she tosses the coin? _____

WINDOWS TO THE WORLD

A fraction names part of a whole. We read 1/4 or $\frac{1}{4}$, as one fourth.

$$\frac{\text{numerator}}{\text{denominator}} \qquad \frac{1}{4}$$

 Read the problem.
Christina is helping with housework. She will wash one fourth of Window A. Shade in the part of the window that Christina will wash.

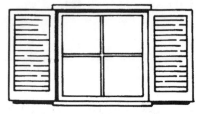

Window A

 Identify the facts.
Fact 1: Window A has 4 equal parts.

 Decide what the problem is asking.
Shade in $\frac{1}{4}$, or one fourth, of the window.

 Solve the problem.
Shade in 1 square.

Window A

Now it's your turn! Use fractions to solve these problems.

Window B

Window C

Window D

1. Window B has how many equal parts? _____
   Shade in one third, or $\frac{1}{3}$, of Window B.

2. Christina washes $\frac{3}{5}$ of Window C. How many window panes are not washed?_____
   Shade in the fraction of unwashed window in Window C. What fraction is this? _____

3. Shade in one sixth, or $\frac{1}{6}$, of Window D.

4. If Christina washes $\frac{1}{6}$ of Window D, and her brother washes $\frac{2}{6}$, how much of Window D has been washed?

   _____
   Shade in the fraction of unwashed window in Window D. What fraction is this? _____

A RAINBOW WORLD

A fraction names any part of a group. 4 of the 8 pieces of chalk are shaded. $\frac{4}{8}$ is shaded.

You can use fractions to find part of a group. To find $\frac{1}{2}$ of a number, you can divide by 2. $\frac{1}{2}$ of 8, or 4, is shaded.

STEP 1 > **Read the problem.**

Pablo has 16 crayons. He gives $\frac{1}{4}$ of the crayons to Angie. How many crayons does he give to Angie?

STEP 2 > **Decide what the problem is asking.**

What is $\frac{1}{4}$ of 16? To find $\frac{1}{4}$ of a number, divide by 4.

STEP 3 > **Solve the problem.**

$16 \div 4 = 4$ or $\frac{4}{16}$

Pablo will give Angie 4 crayons.

Now it's your turn! Use fractions to solve these problems.

1. Singh has 18 markers. He gives $\frac{1}{6}$ of the markers to his sister. How many markers does he give his sister? _____

2. Thu has 6 sheets of green paper and 6 sheets of yellow paper. She gives $\frac{1}{3}$ of all her paper to Hoa. How many sheets of paper does she give to Hoa? _____

3. Mr. Skitt has 20 jars of paint. He gives each group $\frac{1}{5}$ of the paint. How many jars of paint does each group get?

_____

4. Each group of students shares $\frac{1}{4}$ of a box of 24 colored pencils. If each person gets 1 pencil, how many people are in a group? _____

Name _____ Date _____

IT'S LUNCH TIME!
COME AND GET IT!

When you read a problem, you might not know at once how to solve it. A drawing helps organize the information in a problem. Be sure you put all the facts in the picture. Sometimes labels help.

STEP 1 **Read the problem.**
Diego cut a square sandwich into fourths. He shared the sandwich equally with a friend. How many parts of the sandwich did each person get?

STEP 2 **List the facts.**
Fact 1: Diego and his friend shared a sandwich.
Fact 2: One sandwich is shared equally.

STEP 3 **Make a drawing.**

STEP 4 **Solve the problem.**
From the drawing you can see that each person gets $\frac{2}{4}$, or $\frac{1}{2}$, of the sandwich.

Now it's your turn! Draw a picture to help solve these problems.

1. Thomasin has a birthday cake to share with 3 friends. If she cuts the cake into 12 equal pieces, what fraction of the cake will each person get?

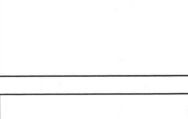

2. Mr. Horak made a peach cobbler for his family of 4. He cut the cobbler into 8 servings. What fraction of the cobbler can each family member have?

Name _____ Date _____

FIELD TRIP!

Sometimes a problem does not tell you whether to add or subtract. Read the problem carefully. Decide what the problem is asking you to do. Then solve the problem.

 Read the problem.

Mr. Shepherd's class went to the amusement park. $\frac{9}{23}$ of the class rode the roller coaster. $\frac{6}{23}$ of the class rode the Ferris wheel. How much more of the class rode the roller coaster than rode the Ferris wheel? What fraction of the class rode neither the roller coaster nor the Ferris wheel?

 Decide what the problem is asking.

How much more of the class rode the roller coaster than rode the Ferris wheel? What fraction of the class rode neither the roller coaster nor the Ferris wheel?

 Choose an operation.

To find how many more rode the roller coaster, you must subtract. To find the fraction of students who didn't go on either ride, first find what fraction did ride. Then subtract from the whole to find the difference.

 Solve the problem.

A. $\frac{9}{23} - \frac{6}{23} = \frac{3}{23}$ B. $\frac{9}{23} + \frac{6}{23} = \frac{15}{23}$ $\frac{23}{23} - \frac{15}{23} = \frac{8}{23}$

A. $\frac{3}{23}$ more of the class rode the roller coaster than the Ferris wheel.

B. $\frac{8}{23}$ of the class rode neither ride.

Now it's your turn! Choose an operation to solve the problem.

1. Of the students who wanted to ride the tilt-a-whirl, $\frac{11}{17}$ were tall enough. What fraction were not tall enough? _____

OFF TO ENGLAND!

Whether adding or subtracting, add or subtract the fractions first, then do the whole numbers.

STEP 1 > **Read the problem.**

Mr. & Mrs. O'Cleary are taking their 3 children on a vacation trip. The airline trip from their hometown to Chicago is $1{,}615\frac{4}{10}$ miles. Where could their hometown be? From Chicago they will fly to England which is $4{,}025\frac{5}{10}$ miles. How many miles will they fly?

STEP 2 > **Decide what the problem is asking.**

Where could their hometown be? How many miles will they fly?
Use an atlas to research towns that are 1,615 miles from Chicago!

STEP 3 > **Choose an operation.**

Add.

STEP 4 > **Solve the problem.**

$$1{,}615\,\frac{4}{10} \text{ miles}$$
$$+\ 4{,}025\,\frac{5}{10} \text{ miles}$$
$$\overline{ 5{,}640\,\frac{9}{10} \text{ miles}}$$

The O'Cleary family flew $5{,}640\frac{9}{10}$ miles.

Now it's your turn! Choose an operation to solve the problem.

1. The family took a bus $53\frac{1}{5}$ miles to the English coast. Then they took a ferry $30\frac{3}{5}$ miles across the water to reach Ireland. How far did they travel? _____
About how many total miles have they traveled for this trip?

_____

2. Colin went to visit an old castle. He walked $1\frac{4}{6}$ miles to the castle, $1\frac{1}{6}$ miles inside the castle, and then he walked back to the hotel. How far did he walk? _____

Name _____ Date _____

FUEL UP

When adding or subtracting mixed numbers, add or subtract the fractions first, then the whole numbers.

 Read the problem.

Mrs. Rzepka's gas gauge showed that she had used $7\frac{9}{10}$ gallons of gas. She wanted to start on a trip with a full tank of gas. However, she had only enough money to buy $6\frac{7}{10}$ gallons. How much less gas did she buy than she needed for a full tank?

 Decide what the problem is asking.
How much less gas did she buy?

 Choose an operation.
To find the difference, you must subtract.

 Solve the problem.

$$\begin{array}{r} 7\frac{9}{10} \\ -\ 6\frac{7}{10} \\ \hline 1\frac{2}{10} \end{array}$$

Mrs. Rzepka bought $1\frac{2}{10}$ fewer gallons than she needed for a full tank.

Now it's your turn! Choose an operation to solve the problem.

1. Ramie is making a cake. She needs $4\frac{3}{4}$ cups of flour but she only has $3\frac{1}{4}$. How much flour does she need to borrow?

_____

If she borrows 2 cups, will she have enough? _____
How much more or less will that be? _____

2. Deanna has $6\frac{4}{12}$ oz. of cat food. If she feeds her cat $2\frac{2}{12}$ oz. for lunch, how much cat food will she have left? _____
Does she have enough to feed her cat this amount for 2 more days? _____

Name _____ Date _____

FIXING UP THE HOUSE

When adding or subtracting mixed numbers, add or subtract the fractions first, then the whole numbers. In 2-step problems, you may have to use more than 1 operation.

STEP 1 ▷ **Read the problem.**

Danielle is fixing the stairs. She has a piece of wood $8\frac{9}{12}$ ft. long. She needs a $4\frac{6}{12}$ ft. board and a $3\frac{3}{12}$ ft. board. How much wood will she have left after she fixes the stairs?

STEP 2 ▷ **Decide what the problem is asking.**

How much wood will be left?

STEP 3 ▷ **List the facts.**

Fact 1: Danielle has a board $8\frac{9}{12}$ ft. long.

Fact 2: She needs a $4\frac{6}{12}$ ft. board.

Fact 3: She needs a $3\frac{3}{12}$ ft. board.

STEP 4 ▷ **Choose an operation.**

To find the sum, add. To find the difference, subtract.

Solve the problem.

Step 1:	$4\frac{6}{12}$ ft.	**Step 2:**	$8\frac{9}{12}$ ft.	Danielle will have 1 ft. of wood left.
	$+\ 3\frac{3}{12}$ ft.		$-\ 7\frac{9}{12}$ ft.	
	$7\frac{9}{12}$ ft.		1 ft.	

Now it's your turn! Choose an operation to solve the problem.

1. Stefan put in new countertops. The countertops were the following lengths: $2\frac{5}{12}$ ft., $2\frac{2}{12}$ ft., $2\frac{4}{12}$ ft. How many feet of countertop were there?

   _____

2. If Stefan started with a board 8 ft. long, how much would he have left? _____
   What else could he build?

   _____

Name _____ Date _____

MATH MADNESS

You can have a lot of fun with fractions.

1 Harriet didn't get this one. Can you? Divide 30 by $\frac{1}{2}$ and add 10. What is your answer? _____

2 Pablo and Harriet are driving in a 200-mile race. Pablo can complete 1 lap in 4 minutes. It takes Harriet $\frac{1}{3}$ the time it takes Pablo. How many more laps does Harriet make than Pablo?

_____

3 Harriet went shopping in 5 stores. She had $1.50 left when she finished shopping. In each store, she spent half of what she had when she entered the store. How much money did Harriet have when she started her shopping spree?
(Hint: Work backwards. Harriet had $1.50 when she finished.)

_____

4 On a shopping trip, 2 mothers and 2 daughters each bought a dress. They spent a total of $75. Each one spent $\frac{1}{3}$ of the total. How much did each one spend?

_____

How could 2 mothers and 2 daughters each spend $\frac{1}{3}$ of the total?

_____

5 Harriet has 3 coins that equal 45 cents. She has a quarter and 2 dimes. Her brother Harvey has 3 different coins. Harvey's 3 coins equal 85 cents, but 1 of the coins is not a dime. What 3 coins does Harvey have? _____

Name _____ Date _____

PENNY WISE

penny	nickel	dime	quarter	half-dollar
1¢ or $0.01	5¢ or $0.05	10¢ or $0.10	25¢ or $0.25	50¢ or $0.50

| 1 dollar bill | 5 dollar bill | 10 dollar bill |

Use a decimal to separate the number of dollars from the number of cents:
two dollars and eighty-one cents = $2.81

Now it's your turn! (Remember that 1 dollar = 100 cents)

1. How many dimes do you need to make 1 dollar? _____

2. A dime is what fraction of 1 dollar? _____

3. How many quarters do you need to make 1 dollar? _____

4. A quarter is what fraction of 1 dollar? _____

5. How many nickels do you need to make fifty cents? _____
   How many quarters? _____

6. A nickel is what fraction of a dime? _____

7. What is the value of 4 dimes and 2 nickels? _____

8. What is the value of 1 quarter, 1 dime, 1 nickel, and 1 penny?
   _____

9. Three dollars and twenty cents = $ _____ . _____

10. Seven cents = $ _____ . _____

Name _____ Date _____

WE ALL SCREAM FOR ICE CREAM!

When adding or subtracting money, line up the decimal points. Then line up the digits on each side of the decimal points.

 Read the problem.

Kim wants to buy a chocolate sundae for $3.20. Toppings are $.55 extra. She wants nuts for her topping. How much money does Kim need?

 Line up the decimal and digits on each side of the decimal point.

$$\begin{array}{r} \$\ 3.20 \\ +\ \$\ \ \ .55 \\ \hline ? \end{array}$$

 Solve the problem.

Add. Write your answer in dollars and cents.

$$\begin{array}{r} \$\ 3.20 \\ +\ \$\ \ \ .55 \\ \hline \$\ 3.75 \end{array}$$ Kim needs $3.75.

Now it's your turn! Write the numbers in dollars and cents, then add to find the answers.

1. Marie wants to buy an ice cream cone for $1.20. She has 3 quarters, 2 dimes, and 7 pennies. Does she have enough money? _____

   How much does she have?

   _____

2. Pauline and Pierre shared a soda and a banana split. One of them bought the soda for $1.87, and the other bought the ice cream for $5.52. How much did they spend altogether?

   _____

   _____

Name _____ Date _____

WINTER FUN

When adding or subtracting money, line up the decimal points. Then line up the digits on each side of the decimal points.

 Read the problem.

Dwayne wants to tie dye a winter jacket. He has $37.25. The jacket costs $28.50. How much does he have left to spend on the dye?

 Line up the decimal point and digits on each side of the decimal point.

$$
\begin{array}{r}
\$\,37.25 \\
-\ \$\,28.50 \\
\hline
?
\end{array}
$$

 Solve the problem.

Subtract. Write your answer in dollars and cents.

$$
\begin{array}{r}
\$\,37.25 \\
-\ \$\,28.50 \\
\hline
\$\ \ 8.75
\end{array}
$$
Dwayne will have $8.75 left.

Now it's your turn! Write these problems as money, then subtract to find the answers.

1. Sayad bought a green scarf and a yellow scarf. The green one was $2.25, and the yellow one was $3.75. How much more did he spend on the yellow scarf than on the green scarf? _____

   He gave the clerk $8.00. How much change did he get?

   _____

2. Jeremiah needs 2 pairs of mittens to play in the snow. Each pair costs $5.90. Jeremiah has $9.78. How much more money does Jeremiah need to buy mittens? _____

3. Shing and Hector bought materials to use on their snowman. Shing bought a hat for $2.35 and buttons for $1.18. Hector bought a scarf for $3.50. Who spent more on materials?

   _____

Name _____ Date _____

TAKING A TRIP

When multiplying or dividing money, set up your problem like any other multiplication or division problem, but include the dollar sign and decimal point. Write your answer in dollars and cents.

 Read the problem.

Cathy went on vacation. She sent 5 postcards to her friends. If the postcards were 25¢ each, how much money did she spend in all?

 Set up the problem.

$$\begin{array}{r} \$ \ .25 \\ \times \quad 5 \\ \hline ? \end{array}$$

 Solve the problem.

Multiply. Write your answer in dollars and cents.

$$\begin{array}{r} \$ \ .25 \\ \times \quad 5 \\ \hline \$ 1.25 \end{array}$$ Cathy spent $1.25.

Now it's your turn! Write these problems as money, then multiply to find the answers.

1. Isabel bought souvenirs for 5 friends from all the places she went on her vacation. She bought 2 t-shirts in Texas for $10.20 each. She bought 3 necklaces in New Orleans for $9.09 each. How much did she spend in all on souvenirs?

   _____

2. The Altobelli family went to an amusement park in Florida. Park admission was $15.00 a day for each person. There are 4 people in the Altobelli family. If they went to the park for 3 days, how much did they spend on park admission in all?

   _____

TEAM NEWS

When multiplying or dividing money, set up your problem like any other multiplication or division problem, but include the dollar sign and decimal point. Write your answer in dollars and cents.

 Read the problem.

There are 4 girls on the volleyball team who need new uniforms. These uniforms cost a total of $70. How much will each girl pay?

 Set up the problem.

$$4 \overline{)\ \$70.00}^{\ ?}$$

 Solve the problem.

Divide. Write your answer in dollars and cents.

$$4 \overline{)\ \$70.00}^{\ \$17.50}$$ Each girl will pay $17.50.

Now it's your turn! Write these problems as money, then divide to find the answers. (Hint: Some problems have two steps.)

1. The science club is going to a state competition. It will cost $750 for the club to travel to the state capital. There are 14 club members and a coach. If they share the cost equally, how much will each person pay? _____

2. The drama club bought 40 props for a play. Each prop cost $3.50. They have to charge admission to the play in order to pay for the props. If 20 people come to the show, how much should they charge each person? _____

TIME TO BUY LUNCH!

A good way to solve some problems is to guess the answer, then check it. If your guess is not right, try again. Use what you learned from the first try to make your next guess better. Guess and check until you find the answer.

 **Read the problem.**
Deidre spent 65¢ on fruit. What kinds of fruit did she buy?

 **Guess.**
A banana and an apple.

MENU		
muffin 65¢	milk 30¢	banana 30¢
bagel 45¢	juice box 25¢	apple 35¢
cookie 35¢	soda pop 50¢	orange 40¢

Check.
30¢ + 35¢ = 65¢ Deidre bought a banana and an apple.

If your guess is incorrect, guess again and check your new answer.

Now it's your turn! Look at the menu to solve each problem. Guess and check to find the answers.

1. Anita spent 35¢ more than Donna. Donna spent 55¢. How much did Anita spend?

   _____

   What might Donna have bought? _____

2. Arwen bought a soda. He wants to buy a pastry. If he started with $1.05, which pastry could he buy?
   _____ or _____
   How much money would he have left? _____

3. Noel bought 2 pieces of the same fruit. Then he bought a juice box. He spent 85¢. Which fruit did he buy?

   _____

4. Mariko is buying a snack for herself and 2 friends. She has $1.80. She wants milk, and each of her friends wants a juice box. If all 3 girls eat something, what can they buy? _____

   _____

HAPPY BIRTHDAY, MOM!

Some problems may give too many facts. Other problems may not give enough facts. Read the problem carefully. If there is too much information, cross out the extra facts. Then solve the problem. If there is not enough information, decide what information is still needed.

 STEP 1 > **Read the problem.**

Jenine went shopping for her mom's birthday. She bought roses for $15 and a vase for $5. Jenine had $23. Does she have enough money left to buy a birthday card?

 STEP 2 > **Decide what the problem is asking.**

Does she have enough money left to buy a card?

 STEP 3 > **Identify the facts.**

Fact 1: *She bought roses for $15 and a vase for $5.*
Fact 2: *Jenine had $23.*

 STEP 4 > **Identify extra or missing facts.**

Missing fact: How much does the birthday card cost?

STEP 5 > **Solve the problem.**

There is not enough information to solve this problem.

Now it's your turn! Identify the extra or missing facts in these problems.

1. At Mama's Cafe, Jenine's dad bought dinner for the family. There are 4 people in their family. He spent $12.50 on each person. How much change did he get? _____

   Extra or Missing Facts?

   _____

   _____

2. It costs $7.75 for a birthday cake. It costs $6.00 to have "Happy Birthday" on the cake. Candles are $2.00. Jenine gave the baker $15. How much change did she get? _____

   Extra or Missing Facts?

   _____

   _____

Name _____ Date _____

MATH MADNESS

1 Harriet bought a hat and a coat. She spent $110. The coat cost $100 more than the hat. How much did the hat cost? _____

2 Here's a deal for you. On November 1, you ask your mom for an allowance to buy holiday presents. She offers 2 choices: She will give you $1 each day of the month, OR she will give you a penny on the first day of November, and double the amount she gives each day of the month.
If you take the dollar a day deal, how much money will you have at the end of the month?

_____

Which of your mom's offers is the better deal? _____

3 Your uncle has his choice of two good jobs. One job pays $40,000 for his first year of work, with a raise of $8,000 every year after that for 6 years. The other job will pay him $20,000 for his first 6 months of work with a raise of $2,000 every 6 months after that for 6 years. Which job offers a better deal? _____

4 If you have five apples and eat all but three, how many do you have left? Can you do it? Sure you can! _____

MEASURING IT OUT!

Measuring is done many ways. Three ways are length, weight, and volume.

The most commonly used measurements for length:	The most commonly used measurements for weight:	The most commonly used measurements for volume:
1 inch (in.) = ├──────────┤ 1 foot (ft) = 12 inches (in) 1 yard (yd) = 3 feet (ft) 1 mile = 5,280 feet (ft)	1 ounce (oz) = about the weight of a roll of lifesavers 1 pound (lb) = 16 oz 1 ton (T) = 2,000 lb	1 cup (c) = school milk carton 1 pint (pt) = 2 c 1 quart (qt) = 2 pt 1 gallon (g) = 4 qt

We usually use only one type of measurement for a given object. For example, if you wanted to know how much you had grown over the past year, you would measure your length, or height, in feet and inches. If you were carrying a bucket of sand, you might like to know its weight in pounds. When measuring liquids for cooking, you use volume, usually by the cup.

Which measurement would you use to tell the height of a flagpole?

_____

Which measurement would you use to tell the weight of the flagpole?

_____

Now it's your turn! For each of the following examples, write 2 units of measurement for each item. The first example is done for you.

	Length	Weight	Volume
1. Your body	inches	pounds	would not use
2. A candle			
3. A thermos full of milk			
4. A truck full of gravel			
5. A juice box			

THINKING METRIC

The metric system is a system of measurement based on units of 10. Most of the world uses the metric system as its standard. The United States is the only nation that does not commonly use the metric system.

The most commonly used metric units used to measure length:
1 meter (m) = about 39 in. (3 inches longer than a yard stick)
1 centimeter (cm) = 1/100 m; there are 100 cm in 1 m

STEP 1 ▷ **Read the problem.**
Estephan and Bryce are using wire for their science project. They cut a piece of wire 200 cm long. How many meters of wire do they use?

STEP 2 ▷ **Identify the facts.**
They cut a piece of wire 200 cm long.

STEP 3 ▷ **Decide what you are asked to find.**
How many meters of wire do they use?

STEP 4 ▷ **Choose the operation.**
To change cm to m, you must divide by 100.

STEP 5 ▷ **Solve the problem.**
200 cm ÷ 100 = 2 m

Now it's your turn.

1. Josh and Mary Ann need 4 m of string for their science project. How many cm will they use? _____

2. Naka measured the length of the science classroom at 21 m. How many cm did he measure? _____

Name _____ Date _____

WEIGH OUT!

The most commonly used metric units used to measure weight:

1 gram (g) = about the weight of a small paper clip

1 kilogram (kg) = 1,000 g

STEP 1 **Read the problem.**

The project that Jeffrey and Gordon are doing needs 7 kg of sand. How many grams of sand do they need?

STEP 2 **Identify the facts.**

They need 7 kg of sand.

STEP 3 **Decide what the problem is asking.**

How many grams of sand do they need?

STEP 4 **Choose the operation.**

To change kg to g, you must multiply by 1,000.

STEP 5 **Solve the problem.**

7 kg x 1,000 = 7,000 g

Now it's your turn.

1. Manny and Serena have a science project that is full of rocks. It weighs 10,000 g! What is this weight in kg?

_____

2. Josefina has just received a present for her birthday. It weighs 5,000 g. How many kg does the present weigh?

_____

3. Warren's cat weighs 4 kg. Leesha's cat weighs 5 kg. How many g do their cats weight in all? _____

4. Hannah weighs 21 kg. Her brother weighs 18 kg. How many more g does Hannah weigh than her brother?

_____

POURING IT ON!

The most commonly used metric units used to measure volume:
liter (L) = approximately the size of 1 quart.
milliliter (mL) = 1/1,000 of a liter; there are 1,000 mL in a L.

STEP 1 **Read the problem.**
Juanita and Raoul have spilled 1 L of the rain water they had collected for their project! They started with 4L of water. How many more mL of rain water do they have to collect to replace the spilled water?

STEP 2 **Identify the facts.**
Fact 1: They started with 4 L of water.
Fact 2: They spilled 1 L of the water.

STEP 3 **Decide what the problem is asking.**
In this problem, "How many more mL?" is the question.

STEP 4 **Choose the operation.**
To change L to mL, you must multiply by 1,000.

STEP 5 **Solve the problem.**
1 L x 1,000 = 1,000 mL

Now it's your turn.

1. James and Tanya have used $\frac{1}{2}$ bottle of vinegar in their project. The bottle holds 1 L of vinegar. How many mL of vinegar do they have left?

_____

2. DeLinda and Jesse filled each of 2 beakers with 1,000 mL of oil. They decided to use only 1 beaker for their project. How many L of oil did they use?

_____

Name _____ Date _____

HOW DO YOU MEASURE UP?

Directions: Choose 2 types of metric measurement that make sense for each example. Use *cm*, *m*, *g*, *kg*, *mL*, or *L*.

1. your finger _____	**11.** a milk truck_____
2. a juice box _____	**12.** an airplane_____
3. an elephant _____	**13.** a swimming pool_____
4. you_____	**14.** a water tower _____
5. a highway _____	**15.** a train engine _____
6. an ant _____	**16.** a glass of soda_____
7. your desk_____	**17.** a mouse_____
8. an eye dropper _____	**18.** a chalkboard _____
9. a classroom_____	**19.** a bathtub _____
10. a baby bottle_____	**20.** a brick_____

Name _____ Date _____

HEATING IT UP!

The metric system has a different scale of measuring heat, too. In the United States, we use the Fahrenheit (F) scale. Water freezes at 32° F and boils at 212° F. Using the metric Celsius (C) scale, water freezes at 0° C and boils at 100° C.

Now it's your turn! Follow the directions to solve each problem.

1. What is the Celsius temperature at which the ice in your freezer will be ready for you to use? _____

2. What is the Celsius temperature at which you can boil your eggs for breakfast? _____

3. If 0° C is freezing and 100° C is boiling, at about what temperature would the lake be good for swimming? _____

4. Where you live, about what temperature is it in September? _____

5. If you were going sledding, it would be about what temperature? _____

6. What are some of the clothes you would wear outside on a day that was 2° C? _____ _____

7. What kind of activity would be good for you and your friends to do on a day when the thermometer reads 33° C? _____ _____

8. Where do you probably live if it's 33° C in March? _____

WATCHING THE CLOCK

Clocks show hours, minutes, and sometimes seconds.
Both of these clocks show the same time:

40 minutes after 3, or 3:40

1 minute = 60 seconds	1 hour = 60 minutes	1 day = 24 hours

Now it's your turn! Follow the directions to solve each problem.

1. Write the time shown on each clock.

_____   _____   _____

2. Draw the hour hand and the minute hand to show each time.

3:05   4:35   10:00

12:30   8:15

Write the answers to the following questions:

3. How many minutes are in 1 day? _____

4. How many seconds are in 1 hour? _____

5. Activity: Using a clock with a second hand and a partner who can watch it for you, close your eyes and see if you can guess when 1 minute has passed. Watch the clock for your partner. Was a minute longer or shorter than you thought it would be?

_____

MATH MADNESS

1 Harriet is having some fun on her day off. She woke up at 7:30 in the morning. It took her 45 minutes to get to the lake and 45 minutes to get home. She spent 5 hours at the lake and 2 hours shopping for antiques. What time did Harriet get home? _____

3 On Harriet's way home, she stops at some antique stores. The first store is 6 miles from the lake. The second store is 12 miles from the first store. The last store is just 1 mile from Harriet's house. If the second store is 3 miles away from Harriet's house, how far is the lake from Harriet's house? _____

2 On Harriet's day off, she is driving her boat around her favorite lake. Harriet makes 3 trips around the lake. It takes her $1\frac{1}{2}$ hours to go all the way around the lake on each of her first 2 trips. Her third trip takes her 1 hour and 30 minutes. Why? _____

4 Harriet was so thirsty when she got home! She drank 1 quart of water. She was still thirsty so she drank 2 cups of juice. Then with dinner, she drank a pint of milk and a cup of tea. How many cups of liquid did Harriet drink altogether? _____

THINK IT THROUGH

If a problem is tricky, use logic to solve the problem. Using logic is thinking carefully about each clue. First read the problem. Then look for clues. Make a table to keep track of clues. Use the clues to solve the problem.

 Read the problem.

Ricky and Lucy both have soccer balls. One ball is white, and the other one is yellow. Lucy says they have to play with Ricky's soccer ball because her white one is flat. Who has the yellow ball?

 Look for clues.

Lucy's white ball is flat.

 Make a table.

Fill in the table using the clues.

	white	yellow
Ricky		
Lucy	YES	

 Solve the problem.

If there is a YES either across or down, the other spaces in that row or column have a NO in them.

	white	yellow
Ricky	NO	YES
Lucy	YES	NO

Ricky has the yellow ball.

GO ON TO NEXT PAGE

Name _____ Date _____

USE LOGIC TO SOLVE PROBLEMS

Now it's your turn! Fill in the tables to solve the problems.

1. Linda and Julio each eat a piece of pizza. One pizza is pepperoni, and one is cheese. Linda will not eat the cheese pizza. Who will eat the cheese pizza? _____

	pepperoni	cheese
Linda		
Julio		

2. Ryan, Wanda, and Sai each read a book. There was a mystery book, a biography, and a book of riddles. Wanda read the first chapter of the biography. Sai didn't read the mystery. Who read which book?

	mystery	biography	riddles
Ryan			
Wanda			
Sai			

3. Angelo, Wayne, and Adrienne each play a sport. One is a right-handed baseball player. One plays basketball. One plays soccer. Adrienne uses only her feet. Wayne is left-handed. What sport does each one play?

	baseball	basketball	soccer
Angelo			
Wayne			
Adrienne			

4. Erica and James both play video games. One of them had $2, and the other had 6 quarters. Each game costs 25¢. Erica played 8 games. Who had $2, and who had 6 quarters? _____

	$2	6 quarters
Erica		
James		

Name _____ Date _____

LOOK FOR THE CLUES

Sometimes a problem doesn't seem to give enough clues. But you can use logic to solve problems with only 1 or 2 clues.

 Read the problem.
Miss Brown, Mr. Green, and Miss Black are friends. They drive cars that match their names. Miss Brown and the friend with the green car were talking about it:

"Our cars match each of our names, but none of us drives a car of the color that matches our own name," said the friend who drove the green car.

What color is each person's car?

 Make a table, and fill in the table from the clues.
Clue 1: Miss Brown does not have a brown car.
Clue 2: Mr. Green does not have a green car.
Clue 3: Miss Black does not have a black car.
Clue 4: Miss Brown does not have a green car because she was talking to the friend who drove a green car.

	brown	green	black
Miss Brown	NO	NO	
Mr. Green		NO	
Miss Black			NO

 Solve the problem.
If there are 2 NOs in a row or column, then the other space has to be YES. When there is a YES in one space, the other 2 spaces in the row or column are NO.

	brown	green	black
Miss Brown	NO	NO	YES
Mr. Green	YES	NO	NO
Miss Black	NO	YES	NO

Miss Brown drives the BLACK car. Mr. Green drives the BROWN car. Miss Black drives the GREEN car.

ELEMENTARY, MY DEAR WATSON!

Sherlock Holmes was a great detective in mystery stories. He used logic to solve mysteries. He often said to his assistant, Dr. Watson: "Elementary, my dear Watson." Use logic to solve these problems.

Fill in the tables. Write YES or NO in the boxes to solve the problems.

1. Kim, Dee, and Paul surfed the Internet using a home computer, a school computer, and a laptop computer. Dee did not use a home computer. Paul carries his computer with him. Who used which computer?

	home computer	school computer	laptop computer
Kim			
Dee			
Paul			

2. Steve, Jesse, and Karim went on vacation. One went river-rafting, one went rock-climbing, and one went surfing. Steve took a canoe and paddle. Karim went in a swimsuit. Who did what?

	river-rafting	rock-climbing	surfing
Steve			
Jesse			
Karim			

3. Kendra, Nadia, and Brett each began a test at the same time. One finished at 9:00, one at 10:00, and one at 11:00 in the morning. Brett took the most time to finish. Kendra did not finish first. Who finished at which time? Finish the table to solve the problem.

		10:00	
Kendra			

Name _____ Date _____

WHO'S WHO AND WHAT'S WHAT

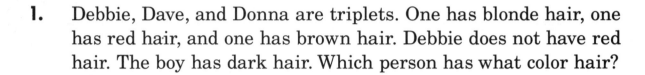

Filling in a table helps organize your thinking.
Use tables to solve these problems.

1. Debbie, Dave, and Donna are triplets. One has blonde hair, one
    has red hair, and one has brown hair. Debbie does not have red
    hair. The boy has dark hair. Which person has what color hair?

	blonde	red	brown
Debbie			
Dave			
Donna			

2. Mr. Jackson, Miss Morales, and Mrs. O'Hara work at your
    school. One is the principal, one is a kindergarten teacher, and
    one is a gym teacher. Mr. Jackson told the principal that
    Miss Morales would be late to the meeting. The kindergarten
    teacher drives Miss Morales to school every morning.

    Which person holds which job?

	principal	kindergarten teacher	gym teacher
Mr. Jackson			
Miss Morales			
Mrs. O'Hara			

Name _____ Date _____

WELCOME TO YOOHOO

You can solve some logic problems by knowing whether statements are true or false.

Read the problem. Can you solve it?

Adam the astronaut is exploring the planet, Yoohoo. There are 2 nations on Yoohoo—the States of Yoo, and the Kingdom of Hoo. Adam knows that the people of Yoo are friendly, but they talk in code. If he gets to Yoo City, they'll give him yoo-burgers and yoo-cola.

The people of Hoo are unfriendly, and they say the opposite of what they mean. They do this so people will not come to their town. If he goes to Hoo Town, the Hoos will give him worms to eat.

He rides his space bike until he gets to a fork in the road. One fork leads to Yoo City, and the other fork leads to Hoo Town. The sign post is missing, so he doesn't know which fork leads to Yoo City.

A native of Yoohoo is standing at the side of the road. Adam doesn't know if the native is a Yoo or a Hoo.

"How do you get to your hometown?" asks Adam. The YooHoo points to the right fork.

Adam goes in the direction the native is pointing. Why?

Solution: If the native is a Yoo, his code is pointing to Yoo City. If the native is a Hoo, he is saying the opposite of what he means. A Hoo would not point to Hoo Town, but to Yoo City. So Adam should go the direction the native points, whether he is a Yoo or Hoo.

GO ON TO NEXT PAGE

SPACE CASE

1. Adam the astronaut was riding his space bike on Planet Yoohoo. He met 2 natives of the planet, a Yoo and a Hoo. There was a tall person and a short person.

"Are you a Yoo?" Adam asked the tall person.

"Dweeble," said the tall native.

Adam knew that Yoos always talk in code, and Hoos always say the opposite of what they mean. He also knew that "Dweeble" meant either *yes* or *no*, but he wasn't sure which the person said. The short native spoke some English, so Adam asked it what the tall person had said.

"He said *yes*, but he always says the opposite of what he means," said the short native.

Which native was a Yoo, and which was a Hoo? How could Adam tell the difference? _____

_____

_____

2. Adam arrived safely in Yoo City. He asked the first Yoo he saw, "Are you the president of the Yoos?" The Yoo patted his head. Adam wasn't quite sure what that meant, but by asking 1 more question, he figured it out. What did he ask? _____

_____

MATH MADNESS

1 The Dolphins are playing the Whales in a swimming event. Points are scored each time a member crosses the finish line. The Dolphins are ahead 7 to 0. But not one man on the Dolphins has crossed the finish line. Can you explain this? Sure you can! _____
_____

2 A man buys groceries at the supermarket and pays the cashier with a check. On it he writes a square inside a circle with 3 squiggly lines in it. The cashier looks at it and says: "I see you are a fireman." How can she tell? (HINT: The stuff on the check is only there to confuse you!) _____
_____

3 Harriet has a new hobby. She collects rocks. She went to the woods one day to find some new rocks. She had a bag of black rocks, a bag of white rocks, and a bag of green rocks. She neatly tagged each bag. Then it started to rain!

She ran back to her car, but the labels got mixed up. None of the bags had the right labels. Poor Harriet. She had to look in all 3 bags and put back the right labels.

But there is an easier way. She could take 1 rock from 1 bag to see which rocks are in which bags. How can she do this? (HINT: All 3 bags have the wrong labels on them.) _____

Assessment

P. 12
1. 355; 699; 81
2. 600; 225; 42
3. Saturday
4. 28 tickets

P. 13
5. ~~Joy's best friend scored 13 points on Friday.~~; 42 points
6. ~~It also has 9 sizes of dog and cat collars.~~; 15 puppies and kittens
7. 1,800 people
8. 100 students
9. 602 guppies
10. 85 fish

P. 14
11. 72 ÷ 9 = 8 teams
12. 16 X 8 = 128 people
13. 16 pounds
14. 20 years old

P. 15
15. $1.72
16. $15.60
17. Answers may vary: pounds; yards.
18. Answers may vary: yards, gallons.
19. Ilda eats mushroom pizza.
20. Alex has red.

Place Value

P. 17
1. 36
2. 224
3. 1,202

P. 18
1. 49; 95; 89; 559; 679
2. 61; 892; 418; 1,323; 1,190

P. 19
2. 6 ten thousands, 1 thousands, 0 hundreds, 2 tens, 3 ones
3. 8 millions, 9 hundred thousands, 2 ten thousands, 1 thousands, 8 hundreds, 0 tens, 0 ones
4. 6 hundred thousands, 4 ten thousands, 7 thousands, 3 hundreds, 6 tens, 9 ones
6. thousands
7. ones
8. ten thousands
10. 1 ones
11. 8 tens
12. 0 ten thousands

P. 20
1. striped flag; star flag; circle flag
2. 52
3. crayon
4. 123, 125

P. 21
2. fourteen thousand, one hundred ten
3. five thousand, two hundred eighty
4. eighty-six thousand, four hundred
5. three hundred forty-four
6. three hundred two
7. 1,000,000,000
8. 240
9. 89,000
10. Answers will vary.
11. Answers will vary.

P. 22
1. 156,823; 16,208,329
2. 8,067; 76,170; 741,038
3. 9,265,081; 1,972,493; 928,492
5. 3,081,056
6. 70,139

P. 23
1. 7 thousands, 3 hundreds, 0 tens, 2 ones
2. 413 − 251 = 162
3. 3,954; hundreds place value changes; 3 thousands, 6 hundreds, 5 tens, 4 ones

Addition

P. 25
1. 56 pizzas
2. Saturday

3. pepperoni
4. $11.00
5. 1 pepperoni, 1 sausage OR 2 cheese, 1 pepperoni
6. $19.00

P. 26
1. ~~Each girl wore a red bathing suit;~~ 32 children
2. ~~His team plays 20 games during a season~~; 9 games

P. 27
1. 70, 50, 120 cupcakes and cookies; answers will vary
2. 250, 370, 620 students; the second lunch period
3. 120, 100, 220 parents

P. 28
1. 6 kinds
2. 9 kinds; yes

P. 29
1. 4 ways
2. 9 ways

P. 30
1. Add; 674 students; answers will vary
2. Subtract; 275 pounds

P. 31
1. 4 boys; 5 girls; 24 children
2. 470 students
3. None (1 girl is a sister to all of the boys)

Subtraction

P. 32

	3rd	4th	5th	total
	49	39	61	149
	14	57	55	126

1. 35 more 3rd graders
2. 43 more votes
3. Bo got more votes.
4. 23 more votes
5. Shay won.

P. 33
1. Subtract; 176 pages
2. Subtract; 43 minutes

P. 34
1. ~~Mr. Garza drove 50 miles per hour all the way~~; 294 miles
2. ~~He has 100 football cards~~; 84 cards

P. 35
1. 1,700 miles
2. 1,400 fence posts
3. 1,600 head of cattle
4. 1,600 acres

P. 36
1. basketball
2. 20 votes
3. 240 students
4. 40 students

P. 37
1. 158 programs
2. 124 bags of peanuts
3. $2.00
4. Yes; $48 more

P. 38
1. $3.00
2. 28 robins
3. 18 lbs.
4. $123

P. 39
1. All months have 28 days.
2. Move one stick from the equals sign to the subtraction sign, so the problem reads: II = IIII - II

Multiplication

P. 40
1. 28 x 2; yes
2. 54 hours; 14 hours

P. 41
1. 200 - 240; about 20 feet
2. No
3. 200 hours
4. 160 apples

P. 42
1. $483
2. pepperoni

P. 43
1. $305; Saturday; pepperoni
2. 2 tomatoes; 1 onions; 4 cups of cheese; answers will vary
3. $105

P. 44
1. Number jerseys: 20, 25, 30, 35, Tiffany's jersey is number 30.
2. 14, 17
3. 495, 594
4. 56, 59
5. 63, 70

P. 45
1. 42 golf balls; 4 days
2. 155 pages; answers will vary

P. 46
1. 6 combinations

P. 47
1. 0
2. 0 + (9 x 3) = 27; answers will vary
3. 15 miles
4. 12 stamps

Division

P. 48
1. 5 watermelons
2. 24 boxes; 2 cases

P. 49
1. 10 holds; Jeff knows the most.
2. 90 laps

P. 50
1. 4 free toppings
2. Sandra's number is 16.
3. $2

P. 51
1. Beware of the March Hare

P. 53
1. Monday: 15 chairs
   Tuesday: 10 chairs
   Wednesday: 6 chairs
   Thursday: 5 chairs
   Friday: 3 chairs
2. Monday
3. Friday
4. Monday, Tuesday; answers will vary
5. Friday, Thursday, Wednesday; answers will vary

P. 54
1. $2.00
2. 50 necklaces
3. $6.00
4. 6 ribbons

P. 55
1. make applesauce
2. 3
3. Neither train is closer.

Mixed Operations

P. 57
1. 33 cans
2. 9 boxes
3. 72 biographies
4. 18 boxes
5. 6 calculators
6. 15 beakers

P. 58
1. 4 classes; 4 groups
2. 7 hot dogs; 2 packages

P. 59
1. $5.00
2. 789 jellybeans; answers will vary